Not of Pure Blood

D0169742

Not of Pure Blood

THE FREE PEOPLE OF COLOR AND RACIAL

PREJUDICE IN NINETEENTH-CENTURY

PUERTO RICO

Jay Kinsbruner

DUKE UNIVERSITY PRESS   DURHAM & LONDON

1996

© 1996 Duke University Press   All rights reserved
Printed in the United States of America on acid-free paper ∞
Second printing, 2000

Library of Congress Cataloging-in-Publication Data
Kinsbruner, Jay.
Not of pure blood : the free people of color and racial prejudice in
Nineteenth-Century Puerto Rico / Jay Kinsbruner.
p.   cm.
Includes bibliographical references (p.   ) and index.
ISBN 0-8223-1836-9 (alk. paper). —
ISBN 0-8223-1842-2 (pbk.: alk. paper).
1. Blacks—Puerto Rico—Social conditions.
2. Puerto Rico—History—To 1898.
3. Racism—Puerto Rico—History—19th century.
4. Prejudices—Puerto Rico—History—19th century.
5. Puerto Rico—Race relations.   I. Title.
F1983.B55K56   1996
305.896'07295—dc20   96-7908
CIP

. . . .

THIS BOOK IS DEDICATED

TO MY MOTHER, FLORENCE KINSBRUNER,

WITH LOVE AND THANKS

. . . .

Contents

Figures, Tables, and Maps

MAPS

Preface

THIS BRIEF BOOK ABOUT free people of color and racial prejudice in Puerto Rico during the nineteenth century required more years to research and write than its modest size might suggest. Along the way it was necessary to learn about censuses and how to code them, as well as to understand such commonplace terms as *household* and *family*, tasks not as simple and straightforward as one might think. It was also necessary to attempt to understand the weaknesses and the strengths of a variety of statistics and how scholars have employed statistics in regard to not only Latin America but elsewhere. At several junctures I had to reconsider and rework the data. It is my hope that this book will encourage scholars who specialize in the twentieth century to produce additional and better data than presently exist, as well as a more thoughtful analytical discussion of racial prejudice in Puerto Rico and as regards Puerto Ricans in the United States.

If this book is successful, it will cause some readers to desire more knowledge about the origins and mechanisms of Spanish American racial prejudice. I am painfully aware that we need a sophisticated analysis of that prejudice and its antecedents dating back several centuries to the Iberian Peninsula. Midway into his classic *The Problem of Slavery in Western Culture*, David Brion Davis states, "In this study we can hardly begin to consider such an enormous subject as the origin of racial prejudice. . . . [F]or the purposes of this inquiry it is sufficient to show that racial discrimination was coextensive with American Negro slavery."[1] Similarly, such a study is beyond the scope of the present book, whose most fundamental task is to establish the fact of racial prejudice and its economic consequences in nineteenth-century Puerto Rico. Perhaps this book will encourage others, including those in other disciplines, to pursue such a line of inquiry into the origin of Spanish American racial prejudice.

In a small way this book is also about methodologies. In chapter 3 and Appendix B, I argue for an alternative way to code censuses for computer evaluation that better reflects historical accuracy. In chapter 4, I propose an alternative method to adjust for undercounts in the youthful cohorts. These two chapters deal with residential segregation and with household and family matters.

Authors who employ methodologies that require explanation—who, for example, apply a statistical method not generally well known or perhaps controversial—face the problem of how and where to inform the reader about these matters. Many authors do so directly in the text, a method that has much to recommend it. Others elect to inform the reader in the notes and appendixes, a method that improves the flow of the narrative and does not burden readers who do not need to know about the methodologies. However, an uninformed reader might place too much confidence in a narrative discussion about which the author has some reservations, which may have been confined to the notes or appendixes. I have chosen to follow a middle path. Wherever it seemed possible, I have placed discussions about methodologies, including my reservations about certain sources, in the notes and appendixes. Books about race, prejudice, and people of color tend to find a fairly broad audience, often even among college students. For this reason, I have sought to keep the narrative flowing, while not depriving the reader of essential information about statistical methods and the quality of sources.

Many people and institutions helped me in the preparation of this

1. David Brion Davis, *The Problem of Slavery in Western Culture* (2d rev. ed.; New York, 1988), 281–82.

book, and I appreciate this opportunity to thank them. Francisco Picó, Francisco Scarano, José Curet, Aníbal Sepúlveda-Rivera, Luis de la Rosa, Benjamín Rivera, Thomas Mathews, and David Stark all helped me in many ways. The late Gordon K. Lewis was kind enough to invite me to the Institute of Caribbean Studies at the University of Puerto Rico. Jon Leong entered the first round of data. Richard White wrote the computer programs and guided me through the quantification with unfailing calm and good humor. Lauren Seiler introduced me to statistics. Jon Peterson and Frank Warren, chairmen of my department, facilitated the project in significant ways. Dean Charles Smith made it possible for me to travel to San Juan at a crucial moment. At Queens College, Jay Gordon took the time for many discussions and readings. Robert McCaa was extremely helpful, and read the draft of an early article. John V. Lombardi took the time in the midst of a demanding schedule to read the first version of the book and to encourage me to keep on with it. Without his good will and generosity I doubt that there would have been a book. My debt to David J. Robinson and Michael Swann cannot be recounted in a few words. Both answered many questions and read portions of the book. Mike Swann was kind enough to take the time to give the final version a careful and informed reading. I did not always take the advice that all of these good people offered, and of course I am the one responsible for errors in fact or judgment that may have found their way into this book.

The Archivo General de Puerto Rico is one of the most comfortable archives I have ever known. The staff have been remarkably supportive over the years. The national library, situated just below, is extremely pleasant. The staff of the main library of the University of Puerto Rico, Río Piedras, have always been very cordial and helpful. The same can be said of the staff of the Centro de Investigaciones Históricas. The staff of the Archivo Municipal de Ponce greatly aided my efforts during two visits. The staff of the Archivo Histórico Diocesano of the Archivo Catedral of San Juan went out of their way to locate materials for me, and I greatly appreciate their efforts.

In the United States the staff of the New York Public Library, as always, were helpful. At the Rosenthal Library of Queens College, the inter-library loan staff continue to support my efforts. The Centro Library of the Center of Puerto Rican Studies at Hunter College is a wonderful place to work, and I enjoyed many days there. The staff of the Newburgh Family History Center were very helpful.

I deeply appreciate the efforts of Sharon E. Parks, Reynolds Smith, and Jean Brady of Duke University Press. The anonymous readers for Duke made excellent suggestions and demands, and I gladly took their advice to the best of my ability.

I wish to thank the City University of New York PSC-CUNY Research Award Program for grants which supported research trips to Puerto Rico.

Parts of this book appeared first as "Caste and Capitalism in the Caribbean: Residential Patterns and Household Ownership Among the Free People of Color of San Juan, Puerto Rico, 1823–1846," *HAHR* 70:3 (August 1990), 433–61.

Finally, I want to thank my wife, Karen, and our daughters, Jennifer and Mieca, for their willingness to uproot themselves and spend a semester in San Juan. Our love of San Juan began prior to that semester, but it was greatly reinforced by our stay. We appreciate the cordial treatment the girls received at the Robinson School. We were all greatly energized by that semester in Puerto Rico and I suspect that it was that energy which propelled my wife on to law school.

Abbreviations

ACSJ   *Actas del Cabildo de San Juan de Puerto Rico* (San Juan, 1945-present)

AGPR   Archivo General de Puerto Rico

AHD   Archivo Histórico Diocesano

AMP   Archivo Municipal de Ponce

Boletín Histórico   *Boletín Histórico de Puerto Rico* (14 vols., Ed. Cayetano Coll y Toste)

Gobernadores   Documentos de Los Gobernadores de Puerto Rico (*AGPR*)

HAHR   *Hispanic American Historical Review*

LARR   *Latin American Research Review*

leg.   legajo

Padrón de 1820   Real property census of San Juan, AGPR, Gobernadores, San Juan, 1816–20, Caja 561

PN   Protocolos Notariales, AGPR

v   vuelta

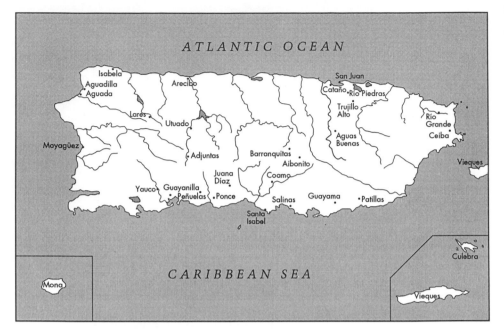

ATLANTIC OCEAN

Isabela
Aguadilla
Aguada

Arecibo

San Juan
Cataño Río Piedras

Trujillo
Alto

Río
Grande
Ceiba

Lares

Utuado

Mayagüez

Aguas
Buenas

Vieques

Adjuntas

Barranquitas
Aibonito

Juana
Díaz

Coamo

Yauco
Guayanilla
Peñuelas

Ponce

Salinas

Guayama

Patillas

Santa
Isabel

CARIBBEAN SEA

Culebra

Mona

Vieques

Map 1 Puerto Rico

1. Beginnings

THIS IS A BOOK ABOUT free people of color in Puerto Rico, a small Caribbean island situated to the east of the much larger islands of Cuba and Hispaniola. Free people of color were those of African descent who were considered nonwhite but who were legally free during slavery. With the abolition of slavery in 1873, the free people of color were conjoined with the *libertos*—the ex-slaves—to form a new community of people of color, or colored people.

During the nineteenth century, Puerto Ricans recognized degrees of whiteness, generally descending from white to *pardo,* to *moreno,* to *negro.* Pardos almost always were the free people of color of lightest skin shade, Morenos those of darker skin color, and Negros generally those of the darkest skin color.[1] Nevertheless, these were flexible terms, variously used. Thus, sometimes there were pardo slaves, moreno slaves, and *negros libres*—free blacks. Moreover, the term "mulatto" was also used. The only term of the era that fairly well defines those blacks, of whatever hue, who were legally free was *gente de color*—people of color. In the United States we have lately refrained from using the traditional "colored" or "black" in favor of the now widely preferred "African-

1. On racial nomenclature generally, see Magnus Mörner, *Race Mixture in the History of Latin America* (pb.; Boston, Mass., 1967), 56–60, and *passim.*; Gonzalo Aguirre Beltrán, *La población negra de México* (2d ed., México, D.F., 1972), 159, 166–70, 172–73, 175; Angel Rosenblat, *La población indígena y el mestizaje en América*, 2 vols. (Buenos Aires, 1954), II, 173–179; and Irene Diggs, "Color in Colonial Spanish America," *Journal of Negro History* 38 (1953), 403–27.

American." For reasons of clarity and historical accuracy, the terms free "people of color" or "colored people" are employed in this book, and in reference to specific documents, "pardo," "moreno," or "negro," unless otherwise stated. *Blancos* is always rendered as whites.

When it was "discovered" by Columbus on November 19, 1493, during his second voyage, Puerto Rico was inhabited by about thirty thousand *Taíno* Indians—Indians in the Admiral's mistaken nomenclature—who referred to their homeland as *Boriquén*. The island was colonized by the Europeans in 1508 under the leadership of Ponce de León, who became Puerto Rico's first governor. The peaceful and sedentary Indians had provided for themselves successfully through agriculture, hunting, and fishing. They soon succumbed to the predations of the colonizers—virtual extinction through forced labor, disease, and miscegenation. The Spaniards replaced Indian labor with African slave labor.

For nearly four centuries, Puerto Rico was a colony in the Spanish empire, the Crown governing the colony locally through a governor and imperially through the Council of Indies in Spain. The island was strategically important to the Crown, because it was Spain's first port of call in the Caribbean, and because of its proximity to the trade routes between the richer mainland colonies and Spain.

During its first three centuries as a Spanish colony, Puerto Rico's economic performance was chronically languid, but after the middle of the eighteenth century a slow and irregular expansion began. Coffee cultivation was introduced in 1756, and it took hold on the slopes of the interior mountains, where it was grown usually on peasant smallholdings. Tobacco and cattle production continued to provide agricultural opportunity, but it was cultivation of the sugarcane in coastal areas that would soon transform the agricultural economy and society. Thus, in 1776 there were only 5,037 slaves in Puerto Rico, but by 1828, with sugar cultivation concentrated around the towns of Mayagüez, Guayama, and Ponce, the slave population had risen to 32,000. With the increased agricultural productivity came greater domestic and international trade, encouraged by liberalized trading policies set forth by the Crown during the late eighteenth century, and consequently more urbanization.

The economic and intellectual currents that swept across the Atlantic world during the eighteenth century affected Puerto Rico in many ways, as in the benefits derived from the Crown's liberalized trade policies. Because of the Haitian Revolution of the late eighteenth and early nineteenth centuries, many French planters migrated to Puerto Rico, especially to Mayagüez, in the western part of the island, contributing to the expansion of sugarcane cultivation with their skills and capital. During this era there was also a significant migration of Spaniards, many of whom proved to be industrious contributors to the economy. When the Spanish American independence movements commenced in earnest in 1810, the colony remained loyal to the Crown, and, as we shall see, was rewarded economically. The loyal colony also benefited from an influx of royalists from other parts of the empire, many bringing skills and capital.

By the middle of the nineteenth century, Puerto Rico supported a large sugar industry and the slave-plantation society that it spawned, as well as an expanding coffee cultivation. However, as the island's economy became increasingly dependent upon slave labor, abolitionist movements in England, and later in Spain and Puerto Rico itself, proved an insurmountable challenge. As Puerto Rico edged toward abolition, the abolitionist movement became intertwined with a political reform movement, which culminated in the colony's first political revolt, the short and ill-fated *Grito de Lares* in 1868. Puerto Rico's first political parties were formed in its aftermath, and one of the sad ironies of Puerto Rico's history is that the colony was moving irrevocably toward autonomy from Spain precisely when the United States shrouded the island with its heavy-handed dominion.

During nearly six centuries, Puerto Rico has been a place of many contradictions: an island of Indian heritage where few Indians survived the ravages of early colonization; a slave society with fewer slaves than whites or free people of color; a racially restrictive society where free people of color enjoyed considerable freedom; a country to many, a colony to some, and a common-wealth in legal fact; an island of grand beauty and blight; a place of large-scale out-migration but also large-scale in-migration. Not surprisingly, therefore, Puerto Rico has been a place of ambivalences, and this book explores some of them.

When I began this book, my intention was to study Puerto Rico's free people of color to determine whether racial prejudice limited their participation in the market economy of commercial capitalism. Almost at once I was struck by the meager number of scholarly and popular discussions about race and prejudice in Puerto Rico during the nineteenth and twentieth centuries, notwithstanding some notable exceptions.[2] Furthermore, for someone whose understanding of civil rights was formed in the United States, it was somewhat unsettling that Afro–Puerto Ricans showed little, one might almost say no, interest in their African heritage.[3] The focus of my attention ineluctably shifted to a more fundamental study of the nature and consequences of prejudice in Puerto Rico during the nineteenth century.

The central argument of this book is that during the nineteenth century racial prejudice and its derivative discrimination contin-

2. Among the exceptions is José Luis González's *El país de cuatro pisos y otros ensayos* (Rio Piedras, P.R., 1987) [first published in 1980, with later editions]. Fortunately, the book has been published in an English edition as *Puerto Rico: The Four-Storyed Country and Other Essays* (tr.; Maplewood, N.J., 1990).

3. There is a small but growing interest among scholars in the island's African and Afro–Puerto Rican heritage. Important examples are Manuel Alvarez Nazario, *El elemento Afro-Negroide en el Español de Puerto Rico* (San Juan, 1961); and Jalil Sued Badillo and Angel López Cantos, *Puerto Rico Negro* (Río Piedras, P.R., 1986), which deals with the period to the nineteenth century; and Ricardo E. Alegría, *La fiesta de Santiago Apóstol en Loiza Aldea* (San Juan, 1954). The African influence on Puerto Rican poetry is finally being recognized, as in G. R. Coulthard, *Race and Class in Caribbean Literature* (tr.; London, 1962); José Luis González and Mónica Mansour, *Poesía Negra de América* (México, D.F., 1976); and Arcadio Díaz Quiñones, *el almuerzo en la hierba* (Río Piedras, P.R., 1982). Much of this interest centers on the poetry of Luis Palés Matos (1899–1959). Newer trends toward Africanism in literature and poetry are discussed in Juan Flores, *Divided Borders: Essays on Puerto Rican Identity* (Houston, Tex., 1993).

ued their centuries-long insinuation upon Puerto Rican society, invidiously producing cumulative and self-perpetuating disadvantage among people of color. Racial prejudice, both legal and social, greatly limited economic opportunities and the possible range of achievement, vitiating the promise of the market economy. The question arises whether this has prevailed in the twentieth century. Clearly, racial prejudice and discrimination, while not as severe as in the United States, continued to undermine the performance of Puerto Ricans of color, and indeed the development of capitalism in the island. Thus, at the middle of the twentieth century, to mention just one example, the Puerto Rican Committee on Civil Liberties noted a near total absence of employees of color in banks and clothing stores in metropolitan San Juan.[4] We would greatly benefit from a Puerto Rican study of current racial discrimination similar to the study recently done by George Reid Andrews for São Paulo, Brazil, in which he documented discriminatory hiring practices favoring lighter-skinned people of color over blacks in service occupations.[5]

To obtain a greater sense of the potential importance of studies about race and prejudice during the nineteenth century, it is helpful to understand what Puerto Ricans have thought about these issues during the twentieth century.

The propensity among Puerto Ricans to set aside the matter of race and racial prejudice is unfortunate because in general it has discouraged people of African descent from being interested in their heritage and from embracing the fight for equal access. The overwhelming majority of Puerto Ricans in the island did not identify with the civil rights movement either in Puerto Rico or in the United States. It should probably not surprise us, therefore, to learn that Martin Luther King Jr. received only an indifferent reception by Puerto Ricans when he visited the island.[6] Of course, the lack of

4. Eduardo Seda Bonilla, "Dos modelos de relaciones raciales," *Mundo Nuevo* 3:31 (Jan. 1969), 39.

5. George Reid Andrews, *Blacks and Whites in São Paulo* (Madison, Wis., 1991), 106–7.

6. Thomas M. Mathews, *"The Question of Color in Puerto Rico,"* in Robert Brent Toplin, ed., *Slavery and Race Relations in Latin America* (pb.; Westport,

concern about civil rights and the absence of a Black Power or even "black solidarity" movement can be viewed positively as the salutary consequence of a society of minimal racial discrimination.[7] Carried too far, however, this valid observation becomes an attitude, even a mythology.

In fact, at the time, many and perhaps most Puerto Ricans of visible African descent did not think that they suffered racial prejudice, or at least not enough to warrant ardent support of the American civil rights movement. This attitude was exemplified by a 1961 questionnaire study by Melvin M. Tumin of Princeton University, who concluded that "By any objective measure, there is only a small and relatively insignificant relationship between skin color and education, income, occupation, or any of the major indices of social and economic position. . . . The majority of Puerto Ricans deny that skin color has anything to do with how much respect a man receives, with his educational opportunities, or with his chances for a job."[8] However, as Thomas G. Mathews noted, two subsequent studies reached an entirely different conclusion.[9]

Conn., 1976), 312: King's reaction as told by him to Professor Mathews. Compare this reaction to King's warm reception in Jamaica, where shade discrimination also was a fundamental fact of life, but where a black consciousness had developed. When King visited Jamaica after winning the Nobel Prize, he said, "I am a Jamaican and in Jamaica I really feel like a human being" (quoted in Colin A. Palmer, "Identity, Race, and Black Power in Independent Jamaica," in Franklin W. Knight and Colin A. Palmer, eds., *The Modern Caribbean* [Chapel Hill, N.C., 1989], 116). As Colin Palmer sardonically observes, this was "a statement that did not reflect a deep understanding of the circumstances of the black poor who heard that declaration."

7. See, for instance, Clara E. Rodríguez, *Puerto Ricans: Born in the USA* (Boston, Mass., 1989), 54; and John F. Longres Jr., "Racism and Its Effects on Puerto Rican Continentals," *Social Casework* 55:2 (Feb. 1974), 69. Robert Brent Toplin, *Freedom and Prejudice: The Legacy of Slavery in the United States and Brazil* (Westport, Conn., 1981), 91–103, makes interesting points about black solidarity in the United States and its lesser degree in Brazil. The relative absence of black solidarity in Puerto Rico can be explained in similar terms.

8. Melvin M. Tumin, *Social Class and Social Change in Puerto Rico* (2d ed.; Indianapolis, Ind., 1971), 245. The substance of the Tumin view of Puerto Rican attitudes has a long history. At the end of December 1873, only months after

In reality, racial prejudice based on a combination of phenotype and skin color has existed and is easily confirmed. The anthropologist Elena Padilla gauged the role of racial prejudice in Puerto Rican social mobility in her 1958 study, *Up from Puerto Rico*:

Much social interaction takes place and many interpersonal relations of an intimate and warm nature occur among individuals regardless of whether or not they have Negro ancestry or whether they look Negroid or white, though there is a stated preference for being white. All other things being equal, it is a social advantage to look white rather than Negro. This is particularly true in the upper and middle classes and is a factor in social mobility. . . . Thus racial attitudes in Puerto Rico involve ambivalences that rotate around the cultural ideal that there is no racial prejudice among Puerto Ricans while social class is strongly associated with race.[10]

---

abolition, the Spanish government inquired whether Puerto Rico had given arms to the people of color as a means of protecting public tranquility. Spain was concerned about possible uprisings by recently liberated slaves. The Puerto Rican government replied in early January 1874 that it had not given arms to the people of color, nor to anyone else. Puerto Rico was an island of "perfect tranquility." In Puerto Rico, unlike Cuba, there was not antagonism between racial classes: "all work together, without regard to color, only to education and social position, and it can well be said that in almost the entire land there exists a fusion of the races" (*Archivo Histórico Nacional*, España, Sección Ultramar, Gobierno de Puerto Rico, expediente 64, "Sobre planteamiento en la isla de la ley orgánica de la Milicia Ciudadana" [microfilm, Centro de Investigaciones Históricas, University of Puerto Rico, roll 164]). In 1909, the colored politician Dr. José Celso Barbosa stated that the "problem of color does not exist in Puerto Rico." It does "not exist in the political arena; it does not exist in public life." Celso Barbosa recognized a color line in social life, but he obviously did not consider this salient. For him, "The prejudice of race never germinated in Puerto Rico" (quoted in Luis M. Díaz Soler, *Historia de la esclavitud negra en Puerto Rico* [3d ed.; Río Piedras, P.R., 1970], 369–70).

On such myths about racial prejudice elsewhere, see Arthur F. Corwin, "*Afro-Brazilians: Myths and Realities,*" in Robert Brent Toplin, ed., *Slavery and Race Relations in Latin America* (Westport, Conn., 1974), 385–437; and Winthrop R. Wright, "*Elitist Attitudes toward Race in Twentieth-Century Venezuela,*" ibid., 325–47; and Wright's *Café con leche: Race, Class, and National Image in Venezuela* (pb.; Austin, Tex., 1993), 125–31.

9. Mathews, "The Question of Color in Puerto Rico," 314.

10. Elena Padilla, *Up from Puerto Rico* (New York, 1958), 72–73.

Gordon K. Lewis got directly to the heart of the matter in 1963 when he wrote of "racial intermediacy, the discreet yet very real sense of color snobbishness based upon awareness of shades."[11] To Lewis, the "characteristic form of racial discrimination thus is 'shade' discrimination."[12] Other writers have found discrimination in Puerto Rico to be social and economic rather than purely racial; that is, Puerto Rican discrimination has been a matter of skin color rather than blood, and skin color can usually be overcome by economic advancement.[13] All well and good, but no matter how less virulent than racism in the United States, the Puerto Rican variety still limited the range of opportunity of people of color in politics, banking, business, and education, and only recently have these areas become more widely accessible to advancement by Puerto Ricans of color, if not so much to those of darker shades.[14] It was

11. Gordon K. Lewis, *Puerto Rico: Freedom and Power in the Caribbean* (pb.; New York, 1963), 283.

12. Ibid., 284.

13. One of the most influential statements in this regard was made by Tomás Blanco, *El prejuicio racial en Puerto Rico* (2d ed., San Juan, 1948), *passim*.

14. See, for instance, Juan Rodríguez Cruz, "Las relaciones raciales en Puerto Rico," *Revista de Ciencias Sociales* 9:4 (1965), 373–86. See also the widely cited article by Renzo Sereno, "Cryptomelanism: A Study of Color Relations and Personal Insecurity in Puerto Rico," *Psychiatry* 10 (1947), 261–69. Raymond Carr, in *Puerto Rico: A Colonial Experiment* (New York, 1984), recognizes that racial discrimination exists in Puerto Rico, but the attempt "to present Puerto Rico as a society with a *severe* racial problem seems to be misguided" (246). Carr views Puerto Rican racial discrimination in the context of that of the United States and the West Indies and correctly finds it more benign. Puerto Rico's more liberal view of desirable phenotype allows for "the growth of an intermediate segment of mulattoes, who once they are 'culturally' assimilated and economically well off, can merge with the dominant white segment to cushion the clash of colors. . . . Blacks are not considered a threat; nor . . . are they bearers of an independent black culture hostile to the white world. There are very few significant African survivals, and such survivals as there are—apart from music and a widespread practice of spiritism—appear exotica, carefully cultivated by enthusiasts" (247–48). One can hardly avoid concluding that Carr considers the absence of an Afro–Puerto Rican culture in salutary terms. He has turned the problem on its head.

and is shade discrimination, a very useful term that suggests a very attenuated racial prejudice, but does not illuminate the problem of prejudice in Puerto Rico sufficiently, that is, does not tell the whole story.

Racial prejudice was manifestly more subtle in Puerto Rico than in the United States.[15] As a Spanish colony until nearly the end of the nineteenth century, Puerto Rico followed Spanish legislation, which recognized degrees of whiteness, or put another way, degrees of blackness. Puerto Ricans of African descent suffered an array of social and legal disabilities, but those with the greatest degree of whiteness tended to suffer the least and had the greatest chance of passing into white society. Puerto Rico's dominant white society rewarded those of African descent for their whiteness. Free people of color understood the system very well and placed their own premium on whiteness, a practice hardly unique to Puerto Rico.

The occupation of Puerto Rico by the United States as a result of the Spanish American War in 1898 subjected the island's colored society to an alien and deeply odious race prejudice that was shocking. In the post–Civil War United States, whites generally considered any person with even the slightest degree of black African blood legally black and subject to the full weight of undifferentiated discrimination. Anthropologist Marvin Harris has observed that we "believe that anyone who is known to have had a Negro ancestor is a Negro. We admit nothing in between."[16] In his comparison of race relations in Brazil and the United States, historian Carl N. Degler notes that "There are only two qualities in the

15. My use of the terms *prejudice* and the sometimes resulting *discrimination* conforms to the standard usage as discussed in Gordon W. Allport, *The Nature of Prejudice* (abridged, pb.; New York, 1958), 6–19, and *passim*. As Carl N. Degler notes, "Prejudice is an attitude, whereas discrimination is an action" (112) (*Neither Black nor White: Slavery and Race Relations in Brazil and the United States* [New York, 1971]).

16. Marvin Harris, *Patterns of Race in the Americas* (New York, 1964), 56. See also, page 37. However, the United States Bureau of the Census did distinguish between Americans who were "black" and those who were "mulatto" (see any of the post–Civil War censuses and those into the twentieth century). This seems to have been forgotten by many social commentators.

United States racial pattern: white and black. A person is one or the other; there is no intermediate position."[17]

Viewed broadly and in terms of the impact of North American racism upon people of color, both Harris's and Degler's statements are correct, although it is worth noting that, as Robert Brent Toplin has observed, there were social and economic advantages to being lightskinned.[18]

United States officials expressed a loathsome attitude toward Puerto Ricans of color, who often considered themselves white or at least more white than not, and therefore entitled to the treatment generally accorded to whites. It was indeed shocking to many Puerto Rican men of color who entered the armed forces of the United States during World War I to find that they were placed in segregated Negro units, and it was repulsive also to many Puerto Rican men who considered themselves white but were not placed in white units. To solve this problem the United States Army created the classification "Puerto Rican white."[19] As the Puerto Rican Tomás Blanco observed during the 1940s, compared to the racism of the United States, "our prejudice is an innocent game of children."[20]

This racism of the colonizing nation produced two broad results. First, it gave new meaning to the longstanding quest for whiteness among Puerto Ricans and exacerbated tensions between those who were accepted as white and those who were not. Second, it discouraged Puerto Ricans of African descent from acknowledging

17. Degler, *Neither Black nor White*, 102.

18. Toplin, in *Freedom and Prejudice*, 99–101. For an excellent discussion of racial terminology in Brazil, see Andrews, *Blacks and Whites in São Paulo*, including a summary statement in appendix B, 249–258.

19. Mathews, "The Question of Color in Puerto Rico," 299–332, 312. There are many examples of the problems faced by Puerto Ricans migrating to the continental United States, even in recent times. See, for instance, César Andreu Iglesias, ed., *Memoirs of Barnardo Vega: A Contribution to the History of the Puerto Rican Community in New York* (tr.; New York, 1984); Oscar Lewis, *La Vida* (New York, 1965); and the books mentioned in note 21. For a criticism of Lewis's methodology, see Susan M. Rigdon, *The Culture Facade: Art, Science, and Politics in the Work of Oscar Lewis* (Urbana, Ill., 1988).

20. Blanco, *El prejuicio racial*, 4.

or attempting to understand their African and African-American heritage. More than any other factor, the nefarious impact of United States racial attitudes caused Puerto Ricans of obvious African descent to disdain association with the civil rights movement and the quest among African-Americans for self-identity. Puerto Ricans with visible Negroid features routinely declaimed themselves to be "Latin" (which they are) rather than Negro, African-American, or Afro–Puerto Rican (which they also are). An untold number of Puerto Rican "Latins" have suffered deep emotional dislocation when, upon arriving in mainland United States or when departing a heavily Puerto Rican enclave (a barrio), they have found that in the great land of democracy they were Negroes or now African-Americans and thus subject to the social, economic, and political debilities—the humiliation—attendant upon that classification.[21] Examples of this prejudice abound, but the following one should make the point. A participant in a study done by Felix M. Padilla went to a white tavern in Chicago during the 1950s: "We were

21. The matter of self-identification among Puerto Ricans in the island, but especially in the continental United States, is complex and sometimes highly emotional. Self-identification often is the result of the intersection of racial, cultural, and political considerations. The richness of the Latin heritage, a desire to know more about and recognize one's African roots, and a quest for the benefits of affirmative action and other racially specific government programs affect decisions about identity. A large body of literature discusses the issue with regard to Puerto Ricans in the continental United States. See, for instance, Padilla, *Puerto Rican Chicago*; Rina Benmayor, Ana Juarbe, Celia Alvarez, Blanca Vázquez, *Stories to Live by: Continuity and Change in Three Generations of Puerto Rican Women* (New York, 1987); C. Wright Mills, Clarence Senior, Rose Kohn Goldsen, *The Puerto Rican Journey: New York's Newest Migrants* (New York, 1950); Virginia E. Sánchez Korrol, *From Colonia to Community: The History of Puerto Ricans in New York City* (2d. ed.; Berkeley, Calif., 1994); Arthur Siegal, Harold Orlans and Loyal Greer, *Puerto Ricans in Philadelphia* (reprint ed.; New York, 1975). There are also many examples of the choice of identity in Lewis's *La Vida*.

For discussions of racial identity in Puerto Rico, see Carmen N. Rodriguez-Cortés, "Social Practices of Ethnic Identity among Puerto Rican Students" (Ph.D. diss., Columbia University, 1987); and Rosa M. Torruellas, "Learning English in Three Private Schools in Puerto Rico: Issues of Class, Identity and Ideology" (Ph.D. diss., New York University, 1990).

always considered black. I remember this one time, I went to a tavern with a friend and the owner of the bar refused to serve us. I said to the guy, 'We want two beers,' and he said, 'We don't serve niggers here.' I replied that we were Puerto Ricans and he just said, 'That's the same shit.' "[22]

Puerto Rican prejudice and discrimination have been informed by a noticeable degree of biological racism, that is, prejudice and discrimination based on a somatic norm image (to use H. Hoetink's phrase) of phenotype and skin color.[23] This view is substantiated in a 1966 essay by the distinguished anthropologist, Sidney W. Mintz. Writing for the United States–Puerto Rico Commission on the Status of Puerto Rico, Mintz observed that although in Puerto Rico "race prejudice fails to show itself in more familiar (e.g., North American) ways, such prejudice does indeed exist." In the upper classes "its baldly racial basis is firm." Mintz agrees that there is much less racial prejudice among the lower classes, among whom "race 'consciousness' is indeed high, [whereas] race prejudice—as North Americans conceive of it—is rare or absent."[24] In fact, Mintz notes,

The degree of race prejudice and the form that it takes varies from class to class. In the lower class, where there is the largest concentration of Negroid features, there tends to be almost none of what we would call "race preju-

22. Padilla, *Puerto Rican Chicago*, 59.

23. H. Hoetink, *Slavery and Race Relations in the Americas: Comparative Notes on their Nature and Nexus* (New York, 1973), 192–210.

24. Sidney W. Mintz, "Puerto Rico: An Essay in the Definition of a National Culture," *Status of Puerto Rico: Selected Background Studies Prepared for the United States–Puerto Rico Commission on the Status of Puerto Rico* (Washington, D.C., 1966), 374–75. Mintz relies heavily upon Julian H. Steward, ed., *The People of Puerto Rico* (Urbana, Ill., 1956). In 1965, Juan Rodríguez Cruz, in an article on race relations in Puerto Rico, used the term "racial discrimination" in reference to the island's free people of color during the eighteenth century. However, by the last decades of the nineteenth century, Rodríguez Cruz maintained, Puerto Rico was moving quickly toward the elimination of racial barriers. Yet, in the 1960s there existed in Puerto Rican society "elements of racial prejudice," especially among the upper class (Rodríguez Cruz, "Las relaciones raciales en Puerto Rico," 378, 381).

dice." Instead there is an awareness of color as one aspect of an individual, with Negroid traits being considered undesirable. But Negroid traits can be completely outweighed by other more desirable features, such as a secure economic position, good social standing within the community, etc. And as such, Negroid features are never enough to insure the exclusion of an individual. Instead discrimination takes lesser and more pitiful forms. The child in the family who has the most Negroid features is often the one who is least liked by his parents and most teased by his brothers and sisters. A dark child may not feel free to participate in all the outside activities of his lighter siblings. Landy noted that in the community he studied, the dark girls were the last to be chosen as partners.[25]

Certainly, to many North Americans this is racism pure and simple. Further, although the "middle class varies tremendously, [it] probably practices more pure racial discrimination than any other class."[26] This is something more than shade discrimination. It is not the racism of the United States, and if the term *racism* is to be avoided, an intermediary term must be arrived at.

To move this discussion to the nineteenth century, it is necessary to explore the term *racism*. Briefly, racism is the belief that a person's physical (somatic) characteristics define social traits, such as athletic ability, musical ability, intelligence, honesty, and whatever else. Sociologist Pierre L. van den Berghe has provided a helpful analytical framework within which to view racism.[27] He distinguishes between racially and ethnically defined prejudice and therefore between multiracial and multiethnic societies.[28] Multi-

25. Ibid., 406.

26. Ibid., 407.

27. Pierre L. van den Berghe, *Race and Ethnicity: Essays in Comparative Sociology* (New York, 1970).

28. Van den Berghe's fine distinction between racial and ethnic prejudice has not become generalized among sociologists. See, for instance, Peter Wade, *Blackness and Race Mixture: The Dynamics of Racial Identity in Colombia* (Baltimore, Md., 1993), 6–7, and *passim*. Wade is fully aware of the presence of ethnic prejudice, what he refers to as *mestizaje*, understood as perceptions of culture as well as "physical appearance" and "ancestry"—and also often understood as *blanqueamiento*, the hierarchical version of *mestizaje* (335–36). How-

ethnic societies are those in which cultural attributes rather than physical traits determine social acceptance and, moreover, socioeconomic performance. Van den Berghe discusses the socioeconomic stratification of a highland community in Chiapas, southeastern Mexico, and concludes that prejudice based on cultural achievement—the ability to speak Spanish and/or dress in the European manner—indeed limited social acceptance and economic achievement. This is ethnic prejudice, rather than racial prejudice, in a multiethnic society.[29]

However, can van den Berghe's important analytical framework be applied to nineteenth-century Puerto Rico? Van den Berghe recorded sharp socioeconomic stratification according to cultural attributes when he conducted his study more than three decades ago. The town he studied, San Cristóbal de las Casas, much in the news in 1994 as the location of conciliation talks between local rebellious Indians and the Mexican government, comprised inhabitants called Ladinos: "Genetically they range from pure or almost pure Spanish stock to pure American Indian stock." The "upper class (called *clase alta, gente bien, la crema,* or *los blancos*) is mostly white, the middle class (*clase media*) is mostly light mestizo (mixed blood), and the lower (*gente humilde*) is in majority dark mestizo or Indian-looking."[30] Van den Berghe does not mean to imply "that genetic characteristics are the primary criteria of social status in San Cristóbal."

In fact, although the town was rigidly stratified and class conscious, wealth and education ("as shown by literacy, correctness of speech, university degree, manners, and so on") were "more important than physical appearance in determining one's status."[31] Indians in San Cristóbal could ascend to the Ladino lower class rela-

ever, he chooses to emphasize the unity of blackness. Wade considers this necessary because if Colombians of color are going "to take proper advantage of material opportunities, black people need a solid sense of their own value and legitimacy as blacks" (349).

29. Van de Berghe, *Race and Ethnicity,* 107–36.
30. Ibid., 107–8.
31. Ibid., 108.

tively simply, as when adopting the Ladino style of dress and/or speech, but in that culturally defined upward movement, "his physical appearance handicaps seriously his ascension in the middle or upper class." Class mobility beyond the bottommost level was extremely difficult for the poor Indian, "so that the presumption of lower-class status is always strong in the presence of an obviously darker person." Just as in the social clubs of twentieth-century Puerto Rico, dark-skinned people were rare to be seen. "At a meeting of an upper and upper middle-class men's civic club, for example, of the eighteen members present, sixteen looked white, only two appeared somewhat mestizoized, and none was distinctly Indian-looking."[32] Thus, it is fair to conclude that San Cristóbal's ethnic prejudice contained a considerable racist bias. Much the same can be said about Puerto Rico. It is more informative and historically correct, therefore, to use the term *racial*, as opposed to *ethnic*, prejudice for Puerto Rico.

It is toward an understanding of the nature and consequence of this prejudice that this book is devoted. A study of racial prejudice in nineteenth-century Puerto Rico would naturally concentrate upon the largest group of people of color—the free people of color. This is especially so in the present case since I am also interested in how racial prejudice affected the free play of the marketplace during the era of commercial capitalism. Such an inquiry would be concerned with those who were legally free rather than slaves, who in any event comprised only a small minority of the population. There have been very few scholarly studies of the free people of color in Puerto Rican history[33] and, in fact, with regard to basic

32. Ibid., 123. On the casino as a racially exclusive institution in Puerto Rico, see Charles C. Rogler, "The Role of Semantics in the Study of Race Distance in Puerto Rico," *Social Forces* 22 (Oct. 1943–May 1944), 448–53.

33. A basic source of information is Díaz Soler, *Historia de la esclavitud negra en Puerto Rico*. Díaz Soler discusses Puerto Rico's free people of color in his chapter 10, 225–61. For the early period in Puerto Rican history, see Jalil Sued Badillo and Angel López Cantos, *Puerto Rico Negro*.

The general historiography of free people of color warrants a separate study. For the purposes of this book only a sample will be presented as Appendix A.

demographic data few serious studies of the island's white population as well.[34] Consequently, any probing into racial prejudice during the nineteenth century that aspires to comparative richness
must necessarily be an investigation about whites as well as free
people of color.

In studying Puerto Rico's free people of color I have concentrated on the colony's capital city, San Juan, but have also explored
other areas. However, it is extremely difficult to study the status
and activities of Puerto Rico's free people of color during the nineteenth century in San Juan or in the island generally. The activities
of the many who served as domestic servants, for example, were
not systematically recorded. Very few people of color owned commercial stores, a matter of considerable interest that shall be discussed later. The area of the economy where free people of color
functioned most effectively was in the crafts, but there appear to be
no guild records extant, and censuses did not always enumerate
occupation systematically. Consequently, economic performance
for the most part must be inferred through a consideration of such
matters as property ownership, size of family, gender and gender-
age differences, and marital patterns. The body of the resulting data
argues that during the nineteenth century the free people of color
were a disadvantaged community whose political, social, and economic performance was diminished by racial prejudice.

The documentation for a study of both free people of color and
whites in San Juan is further limited because there is no single
nominal census for all four of the historic barrios (Santa Bárbara,
San Juan, San Francisco, and Santo Domingo) during the first half of
the nineteenth century. Several of the surviving censuses of individual barrios are in such precarious physical condition that the
next person to read them, prior to some future restoration, will
unavoidably be the last to do so. Fortunately, there are three barrio
censuses in good condition that together cover a reasonably short
period of time: Santa Bárbara for 1823; San Juan for 1828; and San

34. An exception is José L. Vásquez Calzada, *La población de Puerto Rico y
su trayectoria histórica* (Río Piedras, P. R., 1988).

Francisco for 1833. To enlarge the data base, the first *trozo* (administrative unit) of the fourth historic barrio, Santo Domingo, has also been studied, from a census enumerated in 1846.[35] Together the four censuses conjur what we may consider, with some hesitation, a surrogate city. The three barrios whose censuses were enumerated between 1823 and 1833 permit an evaluation of a large, although not random, sample of the city of San Juan's population over the course of a decade. Furthermore, the three censuses are fairly proximate in time to a San Juan city real property census of 1820 important to this study. Because everyone within each barrio was included in this study, it has been possible to produce a broad spectrum of data and yet not overlook the occasional exceptional case.

35. AGPR, Gobernadores, Municipales, San Juan, caja 563, entry 300, Padrón formado por el Comisario del Barrio del Quartel de Santa Bárbara en el presente año de 1823; ibid., San Juan, 1828, Censo o padrón de los Yndividuous que habitan en el Barrio o cuartel en el presente año de 1828 . . . ; ibid., Empadronamiento 1833–1849, Padrón del Barrio de San Francisco, Año de 1833. The census for the barrio of San Francisco is in a bound volume whose spine states Santo Domingo and which contains also the census for Santo Domingo, "Empadronamiento, 1833–1849. Barrio De Santo Domingo, 1846." The census for Santo Domingo is in very poor physical condition, but I was able to work with it. All further references to these censuses in this book presume these citations.

As with many manuscript censuses more than a century old, these sometimes contain missing information, whether because of information unavailable to the enumerator, carelessness, or the ravages of time. I kept a careful log of all missing information. The lapses were few and did not significantly affect the statistics presented in this book.

When the main research for this book was carried out, the archivists at the Archivo General de Puerto Rico believed that no alternative censuses existed. Recently, a doctoral student from Columbia University, Félix Matos, uncovered several more censuses at the Archivo General, and his analysis of them contributes to my own work (Félix V. Matos, "Economy, Society and Urban Life: Women in Nineteenth Century, San Juan, Puerto Rico (1820–1870)" (Ph.D. diss., Columbia University, 1994). Matos writes, "After being told that there were only a few manuscript censuses available for nineteenth century San Juan, I found many of the manuscript censuses I am using for this study" (97, n. 54). Matos studied three of the four barrios for 1833 and 1846, but not the barrio of San Juan. It is pleasing to note that Matos used published and unpublished studies of mine and did so with care.

At times in this book there are references to the barrio of Santo Domingo in 1846, but in each instance this means only the first *trozo* except where noted.

With this introduction we may proceed toward an understanding of Puerto Rican racial prejudice during the nineteenth century, but always in the hope that an elucidation of the past will clarify the present and make racial reform more likely.[36]

36. A promising sign of greater awareness among students and the general population in Puerto Rico was the appearance in 1986 of Fernando Picó's *Historia general de Puerto Rico* (Río Piedras, P. R., 1990, and frequently republished since). Picó intelligently and sensitively places great emphasis on Puerto Rico's African heritage.

2. Puerto Rican Racial Prejudice in Historical Perspective

SPANISH LEGISLATION CREATED and sustained Puerto Rican racial prejudice during the colonial period. When speaking of Puerto Rico's free colored population in 1782, the priest Iñigo Abbad y Lasierra observed that there was "nothing more ignominious than being a black or descended from them."[1] Puerto Rico's free colored population formed a legally disadvantaged caste that was required to function within an economy of commercial capitalism.

Two terms used in the previous sentence require elaboration: *caste* and *commercial capitalism*. This chapter is devoted to a discussion of these terms, which are essential to an understanding of racial prejudice in Puerto Rico during the nineteenth century. Spanish colonial legislation created and perpetuated a Society of Castes (*Sociedad* or *Régimen de Castas*) in which free people of color were legally set apart from whites, Indians, and slaves. The stratified structure of the Society of Castes began to form during the first decades of colonization, and during the eighteenth century assumed, notwithstanding regional variation, a more precise and definitive form. Broadly speaking, there were five castes during the eighteenth century:

1. Whites (including people of mixed blood who were legally considered white)

1. Fray Iñigo Abbad y Lasierra, *Historia geográfica, civil y política de la isla de San Juan Bautista de Puerto Rico*, vol. 1, 178–79 of Pedro Tomás de Córdova, *Memorias geográficas, históricas, económicas y estadísticas de la Isla de Puerto Rico* (2d ed.; San Juan, 1968 [first published in 1831]). For a French abolitionist's impression, see Victor Schoelcher, *Colonies étrangères et Haiti*, 2 vols. (Paris, 1973), I, 314–15.

2. Indians
3. Mestizos (of mixed white and Indian blood)
4. Free people of color
5. Slaves

Subject to differing rights and responsibilities, as well as to disabilities in the case of those beneath the whites, these castes were
less rigid and less corporatist than late medieval and early modern
European estates, but otherwise had much in common with them.
Spanish American castes were ascriptive, endogamous, and hierarchical.[2] In Puerto Rico, where there were few Indians (and there-

2. The term *caste* was used by the Spanish imperial government in defining
its colonial society. I believe that Oliver C. Cox was correct in arguing that
caste has no validity outside the Hindu system and that in this regard race has
nothing to do with *caste* (Oliver C. Cox, *Caste, Class, and Race: A Study in
Social Dynamics* [New York, 1948]. However, Spain, which probably learned
about *caste* from the Muslims (and they from India) as well as from the Por-
tuguese, adopted the term and deployed an imperial system to which it became
intrinsic. Outside the Hindu system the terms *color caste* or *race caste* would
be preferable, but these are self-indulgences within which the Spaniards felt
no compulsion to seek intellectual refuge. Historians of Spanish America commonly use the term *caste* today in its Spanish American historical context
without intending a comparison to the Hindu caste system, which was more
rigid and religion based. Nevertheless, there are characteristics of the Hindu
system worthwhile to consider in an attempt to understand the Spanish American caste system. For instance, the Pan-India Hindu caste system incorporated
the element of "pollution," and so too did the Spanish American system, although to a lesser extent. The Hindu system was also one of labor divisions;
that is, certain occupations were usually reserved for specific castes. This
means that lower-status castes were confined to lower-status occupations. In
Spanish America this also obtained, but only where the system benefited the
white caste. In fact, unlike the Hindu system, in Spanish America, except
ephemerally, the colored caste did not possess exclusive rights to any occupation, not even those of the lowest status. This means, of course, that free people
of color could rise above low-status occupations, as some did, but it was just as
likely that whites would implode upon their traditional occupations. For excellent discussions of the meaning of caste, see Michael Banton, *Race Relations*
(New York, 1967), 84, 142–44; and E. R. Leach, ed., *Aspects of Caste in South
India, Ceylon and North-West Pakistan* (Cambridge, Eng., 1960), 1–10. The
best discussion of *caste* in Spanish America remains Magnus Mörner's now
classic, *Race Mixture in the History of Latin America*. My listing of the five
castes is taken with considerable license from his categorization on page 60.

fore few mestizos), there were, by the end of the eighteenth century, only three significant castes—white, free colored, and slave.[3] The caste system in Puerto Rico circumscribed the social and economic mobility of the free people of color, but it did not insulate whites from downward mobility or ensure them high social status. Several scholars have noted the presence of Spaniards in low-status occupations elsewhere,[4] and in nineteenth-century Puerto Rico there are many examples of whites occupying low-status positions in the economy.[5]

The legal disabilities set against Puerto Rico's free people of color were common enough to the rest of the Americas.[6] These were rooted in two fundamental prejudices inherent in the Spanish ethos. The first evolved from Castile's thirteenth-century *Las Siete Partidas*, which labeled illegitimate children "infamous."[7] It was presumed that free people of color were born out of wedlock, especially those only one or two generations removed from black parentage, and therefore these unfortunate people were considered to be of obscure or "vile" birth. The second was the stigma of slav-

3. Regarding "caste stratification," Orlando Patterson has interesting things to say about the Murdock World Sample of 186 societies, which organizes the societies into four categories. He leans toward category (2) as a definition of society with a genuine caste system, whereas he does "not accept category (3) . . . as containing genuine caste systems . . . " (*Slavery and Social Death: A Comparative Study* (Cambridge, Mass., 1982), 48–49. In fact, I would place Puerto Rico in category (3).

4. See Rodney D. Anderson, "Race and Social Stratification: A Comparison of Working-Class Spaniards, Indians, and Castas in Guadalajara, Mexico in 1821," *HAHR* 68:2 (May 1988), 209–43; and R. Douglas Cope, *The Limits of Racial Domination: Plebeian Society in Colonial Mexico City, 1660–1720* (Madison, Wisc., 1994), 22–23.

5. See, for example, AMP, caja 53-B, Padrón nominal . . . año de 1860.

6. For general statements on legal disabilities, see Davis, *The Problem of Slavery in Western Culture*, 281–88; and Mörner, *Race Mixture*, 45. For the United States and Latin America, consult the books and essays mentioned in Appendix A.

7. John Tate Lanning, "Legitimacy and *Limpieza de Sangre* in the Practice of Medicine in the Spanish Empire," *Jahrbuch für Geschichte von Staat Wirtschaft und Gesellschaft Lateinamericas*, 4 (1967), 37–60. See also Mörner, *Race Mixture*, 35–45.

ery, as Magnus Mörner has phrased it.[8] Spanish Americans chose to apply to free people of color many of the legal restrictions traditionally inflicted upon slaves, a not surprising manifestation of their deep-seated racial prejudice.

It was not until the latter part of the eighteenth century that the purchase of legal whiteness by some few Spanish Americans of African descent was rendered possible by *gracias al sacar* rulings.[9] However, in 1806, the Council of Indies stipulated that it was "useful and necessary" to keep the "contaminated castes" apart from the whites and the legitimate mestizos (here meaning of mixed white-colored blood through four generations of legitimate parentage with one parent in each generation having been white), "and in a class excluded from the public offices and honors, distinctions and prerogatives" to which only whites and mestizos were privileged. This means that practically the entire free colored population was considered among the "contaminated castes" and ineligible for public office. Those free people of color who sought legal whiteness and all the opportunities and privileges accruing to whites were required to prove "free and legitimate descent of four generations." Full citizenship and bureaucratic opportunity thus was normally unavailable to free people of color, but this was rectifiable through the process of whitening, a reality that impressed itself upon the colored caste.[10] Together, however, the stamp of illegitimacy and the stigma of slavery within a society marked by profound racial prejudice were formidable barriers to assimilation and upward socioeconomic mobility.

It is not always possible to determine which Spanish laws applied to Puerto Rico's free people of color. Spanish colonial legislation was sometimes broad in intent and application, but more often

8. Mörner, *Race Mixture*, 44. See also Patterson, *Slavery and Social Death*, 247–61, for a broad historical discussion beyond Latin America.

9. Mörner, *Race Mixture*, 45.

10. From a slightly different version by Verena Martinez-Alier, *Marriage, Class and Colour in Nineteenth-Century Cuba* (Cambridge, Eng., 1974), 92; Richard Konetzke, *Colección de documentos para la historia de la formación social de Hispanoamérica, 1493–1810*, 3 vols. (Madrid, 1962), III, 821–29.

a specific response to a circumstance within an individual colony. The corpus of colonial legislation, especially when codified as in the *Recopilación de las leyes de las Indias* of 1680, was considered to apply broadly. Nevertheless, it is not at all clear that each imperial ruling prevailed throughout the empire. Many examples exist of individual officials circumventing legal restrictions and of colonial governments enforcing Spanish law with varied enthusiasm.[11]

Throughout Spanish America free people of color suffered sumptuary restrictions that must have been especially demeaning and irritating. In the sixteenth century Peruvian free colored women were prohibited from wearing articles of silk, pearl, or gold, and the mantilla.[12]

In 1665, the Viceroy of Peru forbade the black and mulatto women of Lima from wearing silk, stipulating confiscation of the dress for the first offense and one hundred lashes and expulsion from Lima for the second.[13] In 1725, the Crown approved attempts taken by the Viceroy of Peru to limit "the scandalous excesses of dress" on the part of blacks and mulattoes.[14] In 1785, the *Código Negro Carolino* repeated these sumptuary restrictions for the free "negras" or "pardas" of Santo Domingo, and this infamous document now included free negro and pardo males through the second generation of white mixture.[15] Furthermore, free people of color in Spanish America were in normal times not permitted to carry firearms or such symbols of social status as swords or daggers.[16] With such a prevailing attitude perhaps it is not surprising that Luis M. Díaz Soler, in his widely read *Historia de la esclavitud negra en Puerto Rico*, could divine a "sentiment of developing racial tolerance" in Puerto Rico during the eighteenth century because free

11. As in the case of Cuba, for instance. See Herbert S. Klein, *Slavery in the Americas: A Comparative Study of Virginia and Cuba* (Chicago, 1967), 206–11.

12. Frederick P. Bowser, *The African Slave in Colonial Peru, 1524–1650* (Stanford, Calif., 1974), 311.

13. Mörner, *Race Mixture*, 62.

14. Konetzke, *Colección de documentos*, III, 187.

15. Ibid., III, 553–57.

16. Ibid., II, 427–28, 543; Mörner, *Race Mixture*, 44.

people of color were permitted to participate in public festivals and were even received by the governor, who gave them sweets and liquors.[17]

Other disabilities limited the range of educational and professional opportunity available to the free people of color. Generally, throughout the Spanish American colonies free people of color were not permitted a university education, thus restricting them from the legal and medical professions.[18] In some colonies, however, such as Peru, a few free men of color managed to achieve a university education and become physicians.[19] Although also prohibited from becoming notaries, a position of moderate status and influence, some free men of color did indeed become notaries.[20] Positions within the Church were also proscribed, as the Crown insistently reminded the Archbishop of Santo Domingo in 1723 after learning that several free men of color had been ordained there.[21] However, the very fact that the local clergy did ordain men of color suggests that imperial restrictions were circumvented, at least to a degree.

One further demeaning regulation, which may have been no more than an irritation by the end of the eighteenth century, stated that all free people of color were required to pay a tribute to the Crown unless specifically relieved of this obligation.[22] By the nineteenth century the practice of collecting a tribute from the free colored may have fallen into disuse in some places; there appear to be no references to such tribute on the part of officials or the free

17. Díaz Soler, *Historia de la esclavitud,* 249.

18. Konetzke, *Colección de documentos,* III, 331–32. The Crown was not always specific in its use of terms such as *mulatto,* thus probably permitting some local officials to exclude free coloreds at the third and fourth generations of legitimate whiteness from royal restrictions.

19. Lanning, "Legitimacy and *Limpieza de Sangre,*" 49.

20. Bowser, *The African Slave,* 313–14; Klein, *Slavery in the Americas,* 208.

21. Konetzke, *Colección de documentos,* III, 185–86; Klein, *Slavery in the Americas,* 209–10.

22. Konetzke, *Colección de documentos,* II, 237; Mörner, *Race Mixture,* 44; Lyle N. McAlister, *The "Fuero Militar" in New Spain, 1764–1800* (Gainesville, Fla., 1957), 44–51; Cope, *Limits of Racial Discrimination,* 16.

colored in Puerto Rico. This may have been because those who served in the militia were exempted from the tribute.[23] In Puerto Rico free colored men played an important part in the defense of the loyal island, and the Crown may not have bothered with the few who were not eligible to serve.

Notwithstanding these disabilities, the free people of color of Puerto Rico enjoyed a considerable degree of freedom and legal protection. They could travel freely in the island; there was no curfew; they could gather publicly in groups and dance in the streets if they so desired.[24] They could own stores, acquire land in whatever quantity, inherit property without restriction, enter the crafts, and acquire an education, even if rudimentary.[25] As elsewhere in Spanish America, they were required to serve in the militia, although in segregated units.[26] To many, serving in the militia was an advantage. In fact, a royal decree of 1815, precise in its use of racial terminology, stipulated that all colonists in the island, meaning those

23. Konetzke, *Colección de documentos*, II, 334–35; McAlister, *The "Fuero Militar,"* 44–51; Christon I. Archer, *The Army in Bourbon Mexico, 1760–1810* (Albuquerque, N.M., 1977), 233.

24. Díaz Soler, *Historia de la esclavitud negra,* 250–51. See also José Ferrer De Couto, *Los Negros en sus diversos estados y condiciones* (2d ed., New York, 1864), 89.

25. To place these advantages in perspective, see the restrictions in the *Código Carolino* (Konetzke, *Colección de documentos*, III, 553–73). See also Ira Berlin, *Slaves Without Masters: The Free Negro in the Antebellum South* (New York, 1974), 227–28; Leonard P. Curry, *The Free Black in Urban America, 1800–1850* (Chicago, 1981), 16–17; Elsa V. Goveia, *Slave Society in the British Leeward Islands at the End of the Eighteenth Century* (New Haven, Conn., 1965), 181–84; Jerome S. Handler, *The Unappropriated People: Freedmen in the Slave Society of Barbados* (Baltimore, Md., 1974), 69, 77–81; and Jay Kinsbruner, *Petty Capitalism in Spanish America: The Pulperos of Puebla, Mexico City, Caracas and Buenos Aires* (Boulder, Colo., 1987), 82. Consider that in Virginia a law of 1831 made it illegal to teach free people of color to read and write (Luther Porter Jackson, *Free Negro Labor and Property Holding in Virginia, 1830–1860* [2d ed.; New York, 1969], 19).

26. Noel Rivera Ayala, "Las Milicias Disciplinadas Puertorriqueñas: Grandes períodos y el duradero valor de la institución (1765–1850)" (Master's thesis, University of Puerto Rico, 1978), *passim.*; Díaz Soler, *Historia de la esclavitud negra,* 246.

who were free, were required to bear arms, even in times of peace, in order to contain the slaves and resist whatever invasion or pirating activity that might occur.[27] Thus, it is possible that Puerto Rico's free colored men were permitted a privilege—the right to bear arms—that would have been unthinkable in many other areas of the empire.

These fairly liberal racial attitudes of the white establishment were in part the result of Puerto Rico's loyalty during the Spanish American wars for independence, but they may also have been the consequence of demographics. Puerto Rico's free colored population lived in a society in which, during the late eighteenth and early nineteenth centuries, people of African descent were commonly in the majority, but which significantly was overwhelmingly free.

Puerto Rico's free people of color variously acquired their legal status. Many managed to "pass" for whites and were recognized as such in official documents, such as censuses. A few may have purchased *gracias al sacar* rulings during the late eighteenth century, rendering them legally white. However, sometimes whites of the lower socioeconomic class who married or cohabited with free people of color were taken by officials, as in the case of census enumerators, to be colored. Children of slave mothers were slaves, and children of racially mixed marriages or relationships between free people almost always took the legal-racial status of their mothers.[28] Some were born free, having come from families free for a generation or several generations. Some, already free, migrated to the island.[29] Others were manumitted.[30]

27. *Cédula de Gracias*, 1815, in *Boletín Histórico*, I, 297–307.

28. The racial status of a child was sometimes determined by a casual placing of its name in the parish registers. Martinez-Alier has noted cupidity in this matter among parish priests in Cuba (*Marriage, Class and Colour*, 73–74). I have seen cases in Puerto Rico in which the child did not bear the mother's name.

29. However, some free people of color arrived in the island only to become enslaved, as in the case of those free people of color from St. Thomas who were British citizens and were sold as slaves in Puerto Rico, prompting a strong complaint by the British government. Spain supported the British position (*Archivo Histórico Nacional*, España, sección: Estado, leg. 8036, año 1837, no. 1

Some, as was the case especially in Cuba and with variations in other colonies, purchased their own freedom through the system of *coartación* (self-purchase), or had their freedom purchased for them. Under this system, a slave could request that the owner set a fair price for his or her freedom. When the amount was produced, the owner was legally required to set the slave free. When the slave and owner could not agree upon a price, two experts, one named by the owner and the other by the attorney of the local town council, would stipulate the amount. In the event that they disagreed, the alcalde (probably the alcalde *de primer voto*) would appoint a third expert to settle the matter.[31] Once a price was agreed upon, the process was not free of complication. Owners sometimes refused to honor the agreement when with time the price of slaves increased,

[microfilm, Centro de Investigaciones Históricas, Esclavos, 1838–1839, caja 65, entry 23]).

30. Relatively few free people of color achieved freedom through flight from bondage. See Benjamín Nistal-Moret, ed., *Esclavos prófugos y cimarrones: Puerto Rico, 1770–1870* (Río Piedras, P.R., 1984). A broad historical discussion of manumission is in Patterson, *Slavery and Social Death*, 262–96. Terms of manumission sometimes required that the freed slave perform labor or personal services for the former master. On the other hand, former masters sometimes took a special interest in the well-being of their freed slaves. Especially good on manumission in Spanish America is Lyman L. Johnson, "Manumission in Colonial Buenos Aires, 1776–1810," *HAHR* 59:2 (May 1979), 258–79. For Brazil, see the excellent discussion in Katia M. De Queirós Mattoso, *To Be a Slave in Brazil, 1550–1888* (tr.; New Brunswick, N.J., 1986), 155–76.

31. The rules for *coartación* were prescribed on several occasions. See, for example, the Reglamento of 1864, Francisco Ramos, ed., *Prontuario de disposiciones oficiales, 1824–1865* (San Juan, 1866), 164–68. Patterson provides an interesting perspective on the issue of manumission as practiced in Puerto Rico: "Common sense has it that the slave or someone else simply buys his freedom from the master. Such a view, itself narrow and problematic, is true only of the advanced capitalistic slave systems of the modern world" (*Slavery and Social Death*, 210). Slaves in Puerto Rico did not "simply" buy their freedom, since there were impediments, as noted in the text, but the process was relatively simple, which would place Puerto Rico's economy if not among the advanced capitalist slave systems then at least among the capitalist or somewhat advanced capitalist slave systems of the modern world. As the reader is aware, this characterization conforms to my own view of the Puerto Rican economy.

Table 2.1. Puerto Rico's Racial Composition, 1779–1802

	1779	1790	1802
White	35,048 (46.8%)	41,293 (42.4%)	71,723 (44.6%)
Free Colored	31,624 (42.3%)	42,911 (44.1%)	64,578 (40.1%)
Slave	8,153 (10.9%)	13,143 (13.5%)	24,591 (15.3%)

Note: These figures do not include approximately two thousand Indians.
Source: AGPR, Colecciones Particulares, Francisco Scarano, leg. CP.3.

and the process might have to be reinstituted with no sure results.[32] However they achieved their freedom, former slaves were referred to as *libertos*. Everywhere in Spanish America *libertos* faced the possibility of reenslavement, as occurred in Peru during the wars of independence,[33] but this does not seem to have been a serious likelihood in Puerto Rico.[34]

In 1779, the first year for which there are fairly reliable figures, approximately 89 percent of Puerto Rico's population was free (Table 2.1). With a white population at 35,048, the 31,624 free people of color were a near second. By 1790, the free people of color had surpassed the whites in number, and together they comprised more than 86 percent of the island's population. Both whites and free people of color increased their numbers greatly by 1802, with the white population now outnumbering the free colored, but together whites and free coloreds accounted for approximately 85 percent of the island's population. Between 1820 and 1830, Puerto Rico's white population increased to a slight majority at the expense of the proportion of free colored (Table 2.2 and Figure 2.1). Through-

32. See the examples of the *morena libre* Amalia Gimenes requesting a new price for the slave named Gerado, in AGPR, Municipales, San Juan, año 1864, Asuntos Diversos, leg. 24-F.

33. Christine Hünefeldt, *Paying the Price of Freedom: Family and Labor among Lima's Slaves, 1800–1854* (Berkeley, Calif., 1994), 26–27.

34. I have seen no mention of reenslavement of *libertos* in Puerto Rico, but this does not mean that there were no isolated incidents. However, since Governor Prim's 1848 decree against the African race, discussed on pages 42-43, did not mention the possibility of reenslavement among its harsh penalties, we may assume it was not in this way a threat to the free colored population.

Table 2.2. Puerto Rico's Racial Composition, 1820–1830

	1820	1830
White	102,432 (44.4%)	163,311 (50.1%)
Free Colored	106,460 (46.2%)	127,287 (39.3%)
Slave	21,730 (9.4%)	34,240 (10.6%)

Source: Based on figures from Colonel George Flinter, An Account of the Present State of the Island of Puerto Rico (London, 1834), 206–8. Flinter consulted official documents and is considered reliable. I have corrected some of his addition.

out this time, the slave population was still only moderate in size, ranging from 10.9 percent of the population in 1779 to 10.6 percent in 1830 (Tables 2.1 and 2.2).[35]

That Puerto Rico's free colored population was large—indeed, extremely large—becomes palpably evident when the island is compared with other slave-holding colonies in the Caribbean and with the United States (Table 2.3). The relative size of the island's free colored population simply dwarfed those of Jamaica, Barbados, the United States, and to a lesser degree, Cuba. This proves true even when the larger slave populations in the other regions are factored out, as in Table 2.4.

The considerable size of Puerto Rico's colored population raises the question of how threatening the whites perceived it to be. The key to the answer is probably the relatively modest size of the slave proportion, amounting to approximately 11 percent of the aggregate population in 1779 and again in 1830 (Tables 2.1 and 2.2). This was still the period prior to the great sugar expansion, and the slave population had not yet swelled. Puerto Rico's white population does not seem to have been especially threatened by the aggregate colored population. Perhaps this demographic circumstance, combined with the whites' reliance upon the free colored for the military defense of the island, contributed to a racial attitude that per-

35. For additional regional figures, see Benjamín Nistal-Moret, "El Pueblo de Nuestra Señora de la Candelaria y del Apostol San Matías de Manatí, 1800–1880: Its Ruling Classes and the Institution of Black Slavery" (Ph.D. diss., State University of New York at Stony Brook, 1977), 76–85, 101–5.

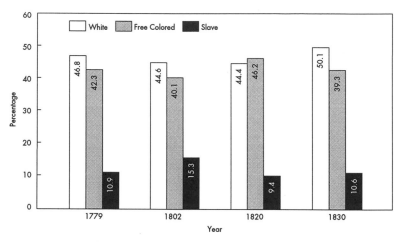

Figure 2.1. Racial Proportions by Percent, Puerto Rico, 1779–1830

mitted the free colored a relatively broad latitude for participation in the economy.[36]

Puerto Rico's large free colored population formed a caste that was itself legally divided into subcategories, which we may consider subcastes, although people could move from one subcaste to another in one generation, and children were sometimes declared to be of a different racial classification from their parents or that of an individual parent.[37] Normally, these subcastes were the *pardos, morenos,* and *negros.*

36. It is reasonable to assume that a small slave component would likely have engendered less fear among whites than a larger one. This would be especially so when the whites formed a large proportion of the general population, as was the case in Puerto Rico. In the colony of Santo Domingo a very different demographic reality prevailed. In 1794, the slave proportion was 29 percent and the white proportion only 34 percent of the general population. In fact, in 1785 the *Código Negro Carolino* placed many restrictions on the free colored population of Santo Domingo that were nonexistent in Puerto Rico. See Carlos Larrazábal Blanco, *Los Negros y la esclavitud en Santo Domingo* (Santo Domingo, 1967), 106–28, 184; and Davis, *The Problem of Slavery,* 240–41; 273, n. 20.

Perhaps as important as racial proportions, gender proportions also affected racial attitudes. This will be discussed in chapter 4.

37. Pierre L. van den Berghe employs the term *subcaste* with regard to South Africa ("Race, Class, and Ethnicity in South Africa," Arthur Tuden and Leonard

Table 2.3. Freedmen as Percentage of Total Population in Selected
Societies, 1773–1840

SOCIETY	1773–1775	1800–1820	1812–1820	1827–1840
Puerto Rico	48.4% (1775)	43.8% (1802)	43.6% (1812)	43.4% (1833)
Jamaica	2.1% (1775)	2.9% (1800)	–	–
Barbados	0.6% (1773)	2.6% (1801)	3.1% (1815)	6.5% (1833)
Cuba	20.3% (1774)	–	–	15.1% (1827)
United States				
Upper South	–	2.7% (1800)	3.4% (1820)	3.7% (1840)
Lower South	–	0.8% (1800)	1.7% (1820)	1.6% (1840)

Source: Adapted from David W. Cohen and Jack P. Greene, eds., *Neither Slave nor Free: The Freedmen of African Descent in the Slave Societies of the New World* (Baltimore, Md., 1972), 4, 10. The 1802 figure for Puerto Rico is slightly different from the one presented in my narrative.

Color gradation was undoubtedly consequential as a person sought social and economic upward mobility in this Spanish version of racially defined castes, and in general the pardos of the very lightest color presumably enjoyed the greatest opportunity among the free people of color.[38] By the nineteenth century, the various racial classifications placed upon free people of color conveyed no special legal advantage or disadvantage, but rather were matters of social recognition or stigma. One must not be diverted, however, from the fundamental fact that being a person of visibly Negroid

Plotnicov, eds., *Social Stratification in Africa* [New York, 1970], 345–71]. There are subcastes in the Hindu system, but these are fundamentally different from the Puerto Rican subcastes because the latter were based on race and therefore were rendered more fluid through the workings of intermarriage (Cox, *Caste, Class, and Race,* 26–29).

38. In this regard the comments of Colonel George Flinter, an advocate of free labor, are informative: "To be white, is a species of title of nobility in a country where the slaves and people of colour form the lower ranks of society, and where every grade of colour, ascending from the jet-black negro to the pure white, carries with it a certain feeling of superiority" (*An Account of the Present State of the Island of Puerto Rico* [London, 1834], 67–68).

Table 2.4. Freedmen as Percentage of Total Free Population
in Selected Societies, 1773–1840

SOCIETY	1773–1775	1800–1802	1812–1820	1827–1840
Puerto Rico	54.1% (1775)	47.7% (1802)	50.9% (1812)	—
Jamaica	19.4% (1775)	25.0% (1800)	—	—
Barbados	2.8% (1773)	12.2% (1801)	15.7% (1815)	25.5% (1833)
Cuba	27.3% (1774)	—	—	25.4% (1827)
United States				
Upper South	—	3.9% (1800)	4.9% (1820)	—
Lower South	—	1.4% (1800)	3.0% (1820)	—

Source: Same as Table 2.3.

features meant legal disability and social stigma; that is, the people of color were, in our lexicon, legally black and, as such, disadvantaged. Furthermore, as mentioned earlier and as shall be seen in chapter 4, the subcastes adopted the racial logic of the dominant white caste and protected their own special degrees of whiteness.

The real possibility that blacks could whiten their skin color, and even become legally white through the intergenerational process of miscegenation, has led many writers to stress the existence of a black-white continuum in Spanish America and Brazil in contrast to the bifurcated racial system of the United States. The racial continuum suggests no clear lines of demarcation between the races in Latin America, and Clara E. Rodríguez observes that "Puerto Ricans share more with the Latin American conception of race than with the North American."[39] Rodríguez is cognizant of the uniqueness of Puerto Rican racial history and the need to consider racial definitions contextually, that is, according to the way terms were used in specific environments. Nevertheless, when it came to the daily lives of the people of color in Puerto Rico, there were indeed clear lines of demarcation between whites and nonwhites, as indeed there were between the colored subcastes. People

39. Rodríguez, *Puerto Ricans*, 52–53. See also Wade, *"Race and Class,"* 233.

of color rarely became white during their lifetimes, and people of dark skin rarely overcame the racially imposed barriers to socioeconomic advancement during their lifetimes. This was the racial reality that faced people of color in their everyday lives, a reality that manifested some troubling similarities to that of the United States.

The Mexican example discussed in chapter 1 is informative also in regard to the question of caste. With independence, the caste system in Mexico was legally abolished, since racial labels were no longer permitted in official documents. Similar legislation was passed in other newly independent nations of Spanish America, but the question arises as to whether the caste system, or a variant of it, continued de facto. Dennis N. Valdes argues that it ended in Mexico City during the eighteenth century,[40] and it was perhaps on the wane in Oaxaca by the end of the eighteenth century.[41] John K. Chance has argued that, in colonial Oaxaca, "dramatic growth and the increased opportunities for trade after the Bourbon reforms rendered the *sistema de castas* all but obsolete as a mechanism of status definition."[42] The large "miscegenated population relied primarily on its economic situation to define its place in society."[43] Rodney D. Anderson has shown that the caste system was irrelevant in Guadalajara by the early nineteenth century.[44] Certainly, in

40. Dennis N. Valdes, "The Decline of the *Sociedad de Castas* in Mexico City" (Ph.D. diss., University of Michigan, 1978), *passim.*

41. John K. Chance and William B. Taylor, "Estate and Class in a Colonial City: Oaxaca in 1792," *Comparative Studies in Society and History* 19:4 (Oct. 1977), 454–87. See also the criticism by Robert McCaa, Stuart B. Schwartz, and Arturo Grubessich, "Race and Class in Colonial Latin America: A Critique," *CSSH* 21:3 (July 1979) and by Chance and Taylor, "Estate and Class: A Reply," *CSSH* 21:3 (July 1979), 424–42. The discussion, centering on statistics, was renewed by Patricia Seed and Philip F. Rust, "Estate and Class in Colonial Oaxaca Revisited," *CSSH* 25 (1983), 703–10; McCaa and Schwartz, "Measuring Marriage Patterns: Percentages, Cohen's Kappa, and Log-Linear Models," *CSSH* 25 (1983), 711–20; and Rust and Seed, "Equality of Endogamy: Statistical Approaches," *Social Science Research* 14 (1985), 57–79.

42. Chance, *Race and Class in Colonial Oaxaca,* 194.

43. Ibid., 185.

44. Anderson, "Race and Social Stratification," 209–43.

many parts of Mexico the caste system did legally end during the early decades of independent nationhood, but a de facto caste system clearly persevered well into the twentieth century.[45] Alan Knight has recently argued that independent Mexico did not "eliminate ethnic in favor of class stratification."[46] Further, "as in the colony, the two coexisted and, while the balance gradually tipped from caste to class, this was a long, slow process, still far from complete at the time of the Revolution [of 1910]."[47] To the extent that one can generalize for a country the size of Mexico, a country clearly of many parts, Knight is as close to the truth as the present state of our knowledge permits. For Puerto Rico the racial situation, although complex, was more sharply defined.

In Puerto Rico, despite exceptions and differentiation within the colored caste, social status during the nineteenth century was determined primarily by race, and the large miscegenated population enjoyed little discretion in the matter. However, as in Mexico, racism began slowly to give way to ethnic prejudice, which permitted greater socioeconomic fluidity. It was easier, in general, to breach the barriers of ethnic prejudice than those of racial prejudice. Nevertheless, barriers of prejudice, whether racial or ethnic, or more realistically a combination of the two, continued during the twentieth century to circumscribe the economic and political performance—and therefore the actual and perceived social status—of Puerto Rican people of color.

Before proceeding with a discussion of racial and ethnic prejudice, it must be stressed that our understanding of the nature of these kinds of prejudices during the eighteenth and nineteenth centuries is distressingly rudimentary. In order to reach a more mature understanding we need both further research and analytical discussion. Nonetheless, there is reason to believe that the Puerto Rican

45. See, for example, van den Berghe, *Race and Ethnicity*, 125–27.

46. Knight is here following van den Berghe's distinction between racial and ethnic prejudice (Alan Knight, "Racism, Revolution, and *Indigenismo*: Mexico, 1910–1940," in Richard Graham, ed., *The Idea of Race in Latin America, 1870–1940* [pb.; Austin, Tex., 1990], 79).

47. Ibid., 71–113, 78.

caste system, legally defined and socially supported, had become, in Teun A. van Dijk's term, a sociocognitive system.[48] That is, racial and ethnic prejudice in Puerto Rico had their roots both in individual cognitive processes and in "the social dimension of intergroup relations and prejudice."[49] Prejudice, whether racially or ethnically inspired, had become internalized in the Puerto Rican psyche to the point that it was acted out in normal intergroup relations. Prejudice had become normative.

Two prominent symbols of Puerto Rican culture must have abetted this internalization of prejudice. The first is Manuel A. Alonso's poem "El Puertorriqueño"—"The Puerto Rican"—published in 1844. It begins:

> Color moreno, frente despejada.
> Mirar lánguido, altivo y penetrante,
> La barba negra, pálido el semblante,
> Rostro enjuto, nariz proporcinada.

> (Color brown, forehead clear.
> Look languid, haughty and penetrating,
> The beard black, the appearance fair,
> Face lean, nose proportioned.)

This was written, as José Luis González observes, at a time when half the Puerto Rican population was colored. It is clear, as González and others have pointed out, that the brown color was the result of the tropical sun, not of biology. The proportioned nose was that of a white Puerto Rican.[50] The ideal Puerto Rican was white, except to someone who desired to be deceived. Five years later, Alonso reinforced the racial imagery in his book, *El gíbaro*, commonly considered "the first literary expression of our national identity."[51] This national identity came to be called the *jíbaro*—the white peas-

48. Teun A. van Dijk, *Prejudice in Discourse* (Amsterdam/Philadelphia, 1984), 13.

49. Ibid., 16.

50. González, *Puerto Rico: The Four-Storyed Country*, 41, 58–59.

51. Ibid., 42.

ant of the mountains, who even today forms the centerpiece of Puerto Rican folklore (and of tourist attraction), not the person of color. The cult of the *jíbaro* was the elite's expression "of its own racial and social prejudice."[52]

There were many opportunities for Puerto Rican society to remind both whites and free people of color that there were differences between them and that it was better to be white or at least as white as possible. Free people of color were constantly reminded of being dark skinned or of being less than white, meaning less than honorable. Town council proceedings and notarial records almost always announced the racial status of people of color. Thus, at the town council, Micaela Vega de Toro, *morena libre,* might try to purchase a town lot; or a notary might record that María Asunción Olivio, *parda libre,* sold a house to Juan Casanova.

On more than one occasion an individual might have to prove his or her whiteness (read honorableness) to the authorities. *Limpieza de sangre* (pure blood) was in theory requisite for positions in the civil bureaucracy, the Church, and officer corps of the regular army, among others. When racial purity was not commonly conceded, formal documentation had to be produced, through an often costly and time-consuming process. A person might unexpectedly be challenged to prove *limpieza de sangre,* as when marriage was contemplated between children under the age of consent. From 1766 in Spain and 1778 in the colonies, the Crown attempted to prevent marriages between unequal partners.[53] Children under the age of consent (commencing in 1803, it was 23 years old for men and 25 for women) required parental permission to wed.[54] In 1805, the Crown ruled that people of unknown nobility and purity of blood over the age of consent must appeal to the viceroy or the audiencia (supreme court of the region) for permission to marry negroes, mulattoes, or other castes.[55] Thus, in 1818, Colonel Don

52. Ibid., 26.

53. Martinez-Alier, *Marriage, Class and Colour,* 11–13. For a discussion of this issue in Puerto Rico during the eighteenth century, see Sued Badillo and López Cantos, *Puerto Rico Negro,* 280–86.

54. Ibid.

55. Ibid.; Mörner, *Race Mixture,* 39.

Lorenzo Ortiz de Zárate, a San Juan alcalde and Commander of the Regiment of Militia Cavalry, objected to the proposed marriage between his son, Don Juan Ortiz, and Doña María del Carmen Ruiz, on the grounds of "Desigualdad notable." Zárate accused the intended bride's family of being mulattoes. The girl's maternal great-grandfather was, he averred, a liberated slave, and her paternal great-grandfather a mulatto shoemaker, known publicly in San Juan. Thus, he contended, Don Francisco Ruiz and his daughter were mulattoes on both sides.[56]

The burden of proof now shifted to the accused. Don Francisco Ruiz, Captain of the White Urban Militia, was placed in the position of having to defend both his daughter's and his family's reputation. The case was heard by the town council of San Juan since contested marriages such as the one proposed were brought before civil authorities. This case disclosed more about the island's racial complexion than the participants may have desired. Ruiz argued that several members of the town council should not be included in the proceedings because they were prejudiced either against him or in his favor. One of those acclaimed to be partial to him was an alcalde, Don José de Rivera, who had been married to Ruiz's aunt. Another was councilman Don Santiago de Córdova, Ruiz's brother-in-law.[57]

Rather than focus upon the issue of *limpieza de sangre*, which he obviously thought he could not win, Ruiz shaped his rebuttal around the question of unequal partners. Indeed, he considered the children and families to be equal. Both he and his brother, an honorary royal official, had been alcaldes, and their nearest relatives were married to a lieutenant colonel, to captains, and to many others of note. Turning to Zárate's family, he did not think that he would at the moment consider the matter of their defects, which they may or may not have had; rather, he challenged the charge of inequality on two grounds. The first was that his and Zárate's wife were re-

56. AGPR, Ayuntamiento de San Juan, Asuntos Diversos, año 1818, leg. 21, "Expediente que contiene el informe sobre los antecedentes del alferez de fragata Dn Juan Ortiz de Zarate."
57. Ibid.

lated. Less dramatic but perhaps more interesting was the second: that they were all natives of the island; that there were neither titles of Castile nor a class of *encomenderos* (holders of grants of Indian labor who in the sixteenth century sometimes approached the status of nobility) in the island; and that the suggested inequality was imaginary.[58] Ruiz was really postulating the existence of a new race in Puerto Rico, one that would honor deed rather than bloodlines. Unfortunately, the disposition of the Zárate-Ruiz case has not been located. Although Ruiz's conception of racial equality may have been a dream, it is doubtful that he or many others were social democrats. In 1825, for instance, Don Santiago Labiosa opposed the intended marriage between his son, Don José Bernardo, and María Teresa Masabe, on the grounds that she was a former slave, a *parda liberta*. After considering the bloodlines of both parties, the audiencia ruled in the father's favor, opposing the marriage.[59]

Marriage to a person of color also carried with it liability. In 1806, Don Manuel Hernáiz purchased at public auction the position of alderman-chief constable (*regidor–alguacil mayor*) on the town council of San Juan. Opposition to admitting Hernáiz existed within the council on the grounds that his wife was "notoriously parda."[60] In supporting the movement against Hernáiz, the city's attorney observed in October that although Miguel Henrique, the celebrated mulatto shoemaker, was honored by the Crown by being granted use of the honorific "don" and the title of captain, as well as a gold medal emblazoned with the royal effigy, he was not extricated from his mulatto class and condition. Thus, Hernáiz's wife could not transcend her class or condition. Obviously, at this high level of "white" society, racism, pure and straightforward, rather

58. Ibid.

59. AGPR, Gobernadores, Audiencia, año 1825, caja 292, "Expediente sobre el auto . . . declarando justa la oposición de D. Santiago Labiosa a prestar su consentimiento al matrimonio que su hijo D. José Bernardo trataba de contratar con la parda liberta María Teresa Masave." Note that the audiencia chose to deprive the young lady of the honorific title *doña*.

60. *ACSJ*, vol. 1803–1809, 222–25.

than van den Berghe's ethnic prejudice or Lewis's shade discrimination, was the characteristic prejudice. This was a racism that sustained ascriptive castes.

But the city's attorney was not through. As another example he noted two additional pardos, José Antonio Ylarraza and Dionisio Antonio Peñalvers, also distinguished, whose descendants, although of legitimate birth, had never aspired to positions of honor or to marriage with whites.[61] Upon hearing the attorney's opinion, one councilman referred to Hernáiz's attempt to enter the council as "rash, injust and even scandalous."[62] Clearly, it was not helpful to be married to a family of color. However, and this is extremely important, Hernáiz was not removed from his purchased position. It is not clear whether the royal bureaucracy had moved toward a more liberal racial policy or wanted to preserve the validity of vendible bureaucratic positions. In 1825, when no saleable position was at stake, the bureaucracy reverted to its traditional illiberál policy. As we have seen, in that year, Don Santiago Labiosa opposed the intended marriage between his son Don José Bernardo and María Masabe on the grounds that she was a former slave, and the audiencia ruled in the father's favor, opposing the marriage.[63] In any event, the needs of the government were beginning to set a limit to Puerto Rican racism.

This limit is exemplified in another case involving the attitude of San Juan's leading citizens toward people of color. In 1809, Don Tiburcio Durán Villafañe purchased a seat on the town council. There was strong support for him among the councilmen. It was noted that he was a captain of the urban militia of Caguas and was linked by marriage to the island's leading families. However, one of the two alcaldes objected to Villafañe's attempt to secure a position on the council because of a public rumor that he was not of com-

61. Ibid., 281–85.
62. Ibid.
63. AGPR, Gobernadores, Audiencia, año 1825, caja 292, "Expediente sobre el auto . . . declarando justa la oposición de D. Santiago Labiosa a prestar su consentimiento al matrimonio que su hijo D. José Bernardo trataba de contratar con la parda liberta María Teresa Masave."

pletely pure blood—*limpieza de sangre*; that is, he was not completely white.[64] Thus, "tainted" blood was held a serious enough liability that merely the rumor of it might deprive one of access to a position on the capital's town council. Interesting also is that to the degree that people were correct about Villafañe's racial heritage, the island's leading families had African blood running through their veins. Furthermore, one councilman was denied a vote in the matter because he was related to Villafañe![65]

The Villafañe matter also may have revealed more than the town councilmen intended. In the following month the case was considered again, and this time another councilman seized upon the racial issue. Don José María Dávila opposed Villafañe because he had always heard from his elders that the Villafañe family were mulattoes, which was supported by public knowledge, he asserted. Further, a cavalry unit refused to admit to a rank of distinction one or two of Villafañe's sons, a repulse that he suffered and consented to, according to the councilman. Dávila even questioned the validity of any document of pure blood that Villafañe might have presented. Indeed, Dávila was adamant: public interest would be damaged if the town council admitted a man who was perceived publicly to be a mulatto. His case against Villafañe was not enough to satisfy Dávila. He also challenged the vote of two other members of the council—the vote of a councilman on the grounds that he was married to a relative of Villafañe's, and the vote of an alcalde because he was related at the third degree to Villafañe's wife. Dávila also wanted the vote of another councilman voided if it were demonstrated that he too was related to a prohibited degree (this prohibition not having to do with pureness of blood).[66] This certainly did not leave many members of the town council untainted. Interestingly, in 1810 the audiencia ruled in favor of Villafañe.[67] Again,

64. *ACSJ*, vol. 1803–1809, 72–76.

65. Ibid.

66. Ibid., 81–84. Dávila's argument was supported by Don Francisco Dávila, alcalde, who had earlier opposed Villafañe. Again he invoked rumor: his father constantly tells him that those with the name Villafañe are not of pure blood, something believed generally, he thought (Ibid.).

67. Ibid.

and for whatever reason, we see the royal bureaucracy assuming a more racially tolerant stance than that of the island's white establishment. However, this does not mean that racism had become deinstitutionalized, for this was not the case.

That free people of African descent who had not passed into the white establishment were reminded of their lesser place in society can be seen in three especially important government documents. The first is the 1812 Constitution of Cádiz. This constitution was drawn and promulgated by the *Cortes*, the parliament sitting in Cádiz, Spain in flight from the French invaders and loyal to King Ferdinand VII, who had been deposed by Napoleon in 1808 and replaced by Napoleon's brother Joseph. The constitution was the governing organic code for Spanish-controlled Spain and for the colonies. The delegates to the *Cortes* at Cádiz faced many dilemmas, one of which was how to evaluate colonial representation in the *Cortes*. If people of color were included in determining representation, the colonies would have had greater representation in the *Cortes* than would Spain. Article 5 of the constitution declared that all men born and resident in Spanish territory were Spaniards, including freed slaves. However, Article 22 of the constitution solved the problem of representation from the Spanish point of view by excluding from citizenship the colored castes, which meant that free people of color could not vote in elections or be counted for the purpose of determining representation in future parliaments. Furthermore, Article 23 prohibited the colored castes, as noncitizens, from holding municipal positions.[68]

The second document is the famous *Cédula de Gracias* of 1815, the Crown's attempt to reward the inhabitants of Puerto Rico for their service and loyalty during the early wars of independence by liberalizing trade and stimulating the island's economy.[69] As part of this liberal and stimulating policy, migration of both whites *and* free people of color to Puerto Rico was encouraged, with each colo-

68. See the impassioned discussion by Isabelo Zenon Cruz, *Narciso descubre su trasero: El negro en la cultura Puertorriqueña* (2d. ed.; Humacao, P.R., 1975), I, 25–28.

69. *Cédula de Gracias*, in *Boletín Histórico*, I, 297–307.

nist being granted a standard amount of land on which to settle. White colonists of either sex who brought slaves with them received additional allotments for each slave equal to one-half their own allotment. Free people of color who were heads of families were granted the same amount of land that was calculated for slaves.[70] Further, if the free people of color brought slaves with them, they too received additional land allotments, but equal to one-half that which was calculated for slaves accompanying whites. Thus, not only were free colored immigrants—although clearly welcome by the Crown to settle in Puerto Rico—discriminated against with regard to white immigrants, their slaves counted for less in the matter of land allotments than did the slaves of white immigrants.[71]

The third document was Governor Prim's infamous decree against the African race, promulgated at the end of May 1848. Any free person of color who had considered racial prejudice and its consequence merely a matter of "ethnic" or "shade" discrimination, a sometimes bother in an otherwise open society, must now have had second thoughts. Upon learning of the destructive activities of the ex-slaves recently liberated by the French in Martinique and Guadeloupe, and considering the "ferocious stupidity of the African race," Governor Prim determined to lessen the possibility of similar uprisings in Puerto Rico.[72] All crimes committed by people of the African race, be they free or slave, would henceforth be judged by a military court. Any free colored person who used arms against a white person, no matter if justified, would have his right hand cut off. In the event that the white person was

70. Ibid., articles 10 and 11.

71. José Luis González argues that "the main objective of the *Real Cédula de Gracias* of 1815 was to 'whiten' Puerto Rican society" (*Puerto Rico: The Four Storyed Country*, 35–36). I believe that he is completely mistaken.

72. "Bando del General Prim contra la raza Africana," Cayetano Coll y Toste, *Historia de la esclavitud en Puerto Rico* (San Juan, 1969), 79–85. There was in fact a tradition of slave uprisings in Puerto Rico. See Guillermo A. Baralt, *Esclavos rebeldes: Conspiraciones y sublevaciones de esclavos en Puerto Rico (1795–1873)* (San Juan, 1981), *passim*.

wounded, the person of color would be executed by firing squad. Any person of color who insulted a white by word, or maltreated or threatened him in any way, would be tried and sentenced according to circumstances. If two or more people of color were to fight in the streets or other public places, using only their hands, they would be sentenced to 15 days of work on public roads or be required to pay a fine of 25 pesos. If any of the combatants used stick or stone, with minor wounds resulting, the penalty would be a month's work on the roads or a fine of 50 pesos. However, if the wounds were grave, the penalty would be four years of incarceration. In the event that firearms were used, the penalties were more severe.[73] This virulent document was short-lived: a new governor, Juan de la Pezuela, rescinded it in November.[74] Nevertheless, one wonders what emotional impact it had upon the island's free people of color.

Prim's decree may be taken as the nadir of racially inspired prejudice and discrimination in Puerto Rico during the nineteenth century. The island's free colored population had lived in a society much more racially tolerant than the 1848 decree might make it seem. This is precisely the point, however. To people like Prim the free people of color were of the "African race" and therefore subject to extreme forms of discrimination. This was racism, pure and simple, and ugly. Other Puerto Ricans and other royal bureaucrats, however, had moved far from this primitive racism toward a more benign "ethnic" or "shade" discrimination that offered clear rewards for whiteness.

In fact, Puerto Rico's free people of color were provided with an impressive degree of legal protection, notwithstanding the possibility of reversals, as was the case in 1848. Two legal rights were especially important and were fundamental to their participation in the market economy. Puerto Rico's free people of color, male and female, had access to the courts and to the town councils. For the

73. Coll y Toste, *Historia de la esclavitud,* 79–85. I have mentioned only the penalties relating to free people of color. Slaves were assigned separate penalties.

74. "Bando del Gobernador Pezuela," ibid., 89–91.

great majority of the island's general population the most important courts were the small claims courts. These were divided into
two categories: *Juicios Verbales* and *Paz y Conciliación*. All civil
cases involving sums of less than 400 pesos were heard by the local
alcaldes and were resolved verbally. In the absence of resolution,
the litigation was raised to a higher level, *Paz y Conciliación*, for
adjudication. It was at the small claims level that most artisans,
storekeepers, and the rest of the population would have taken their
legal problems involving money.[75] At the town council the free
person of color could appear in person to request the purchase or
rental of a piece of land owned by the town, for instance, or a group
of them might appear to redress a labor grievance.[76] In both instances, these were legal rights of no small importance.

What does this mean, discrimination *and* rights? It means that
although some Puerto Ricans and Spanish bureaucrats were still

75. The records for San Juan that still exist, as well as those for other parts of
the island (AGPR, Tribunales), generally do not refer to the race of the participants, a healthy sign, but one which eliminates the possibility of examining
these valuable records for patterns of race and possibly racism.

76. Examples of such access to a town council may be seen in any volume of
the era in *ACSJ*. Two other institutions of importance offered access to people of
color. The lay sodalities, *cofradías*, in some parts of Latin America comprised
slaves or free coloreds exclusively. They offered financial and spiritual aid to
their members and families. Unfortunately, very few records of the sodalities
exist or have yet been found for San Juan. A sodality created in the Convent of
San Francisco in San Juan by royal decree of 1826 stated that all principal brothers and sisters must be white and that all minor brothers and sisters could be of
any race (AHD, Gobierno, Asociaciones, 1826–1966, G-114). Thus, people of
color had access to potential spiritual and financial support, but from a subordinate position. Perhaps someday we will be able to learn more about the *cofradías* and the place of the free people of color within them.

The masonic lodges, established during the nineteenth century in many
parts of the island, were supposed to admit without regard to color, but there is
reason to believe that they did not always do so. On the other hand, members
were not classified according to race or color, a liberal attitude but one that
greatly lessens the likelihood that we shall ever learn much about the inter-
nal racial practices of the masonic lodges (José Antonio Ayala, *La masonería
de obediencia Española en Puerto Rico en el siglo XIX* [Murcia, Spain, 1991],
184–89).

rooted in racism and its derivative prejudice, during the nineteenth century there was also a movement toward broad acceptance and legal protection of free people of color. The prejudice of the nineteenth century was not fully van den Berghe's ethnic or Lewis's shade discrimination, although clearly there was movement in these directions in the prevailing attitudes of many. Racial prejudice and discrimination in nineteenth-century Puerto Rico were more complex and forgiving than their counterparts in the United States, and did not prepare Puerto Ricans of color for their confrontation with Anglo-Saxon domination. It is in this context that we see the significance of van den Berghe's and Lewis's taxonomic refinements. By the end of the nineteenth century, Puerto Rican racial prejudice had evolved away from biological racism toward a more culturally centered prejudice.

On the other hand, in the United States during the twentieth century, racism has been essentially biological. The white establishment in the United States has conflated African-Americans into one racial group not only when discriminating, but also when attempting to reform. Terms such as *ethnic prejudice* and *shade discrimination* are not evocative enough for us as we attempt to remake our society in a fundamental way and, in the United States context, would be insulting to those who have suffered what we call *racism*. But to the Puerto Rican mind the prejudice seen or suffered in the island was and is not the racism experienced in the United States, and this is true. It is no wonder that many Puerto Ricans with Negroid features attempt to distance themselves from United States racism by denying their African genealogy. For example, this is why the United States census of 1950 could report that of the 250,000 Puerto Ricans in New York City, 92 percent were white and only 8 percent nonwhite; and that in 1960, of the 612,000 Puerto Ricans in the city, 96 percent were white.[77] One way to deny

77. Joseph P. Fitzpatrick, *Puerto Rican Americans* (2d ed., Englewood Cliffs, N.J., 1987), 110. For 1970 and 1980, see Rodríguez, *Puerto Ricans*, 63–66. The 1980 census included the "Hispanic" category, and in New York City "Less than 4% of Puerto Ricans . . . identified as Black, only 44% as White, and the remainder (48%) as 'Other' and wrote in a Spanish descriptor--Puerto Rican,

African heritage is of course cosmetic, but another way is to pro-
claim an Indian genealogy. Never mind that the island contained
precious few Indians by the eighteenth century. Thus, it has been
suggested humorously that there are more Indians in Puerto Rico
now than in the time of Columbus.[78]

The final term that requires explanation is *capitalism*. It is important to understand the nature of Puerto Rico's colonial economy
in order to understand the economic context in which the free people of color functioned. Terms such as *feudalism, mercantilism*,
and *capitalism*, among a long list of others, possess the powerful
capacity to order our thoughts and define the manner in which we
look at historical developments. Indeed, any terminological definition of Puerto Rico's economy will affect our evaluation of the
economic performance of the free people of color. For this reason, the colonial economy will be defined, and some of the consequences of that definition explored.

The Spanish American colonial economy, at least by the middle
of the eighteenth century, was fundamentally one of preindustrial
commercial capitalism. The colonial economy and subsequently
the national economies were to varying degrees based on money,
exchange, private property, and the profit motive.[79] John K. Chance

---

Boricua, Hispanic, or the like" (64). Thus, as Clara Rodríguez observes, black
Puerto Ricans chose not to identify—that is, assimilate—with the black community. Further, many chose not to identify with the white community either,
in both instances preferring to assert their Hispanic heritage (64).

78. I have paraphrased Mathews, "The Question of Color in Puerto Rico,"
317. It is humor that has not yet worn thin. In this regard, the experience of
Peter Wade, who studied racism in modern Colombia, is of interest. In Mede-
llín, Wade came to know a woman whose mother appeared in a picture to be
classifiable by many Colombians as black. He asked his friend if her mother had
been a *negra*? "No, more like an Indian." He later spoke to a black woman who
had known his friend's mother and inquired about the matter. "She was as black
as I am; it's just that her children came out white, so they don't like to admit it"
(Peter Wade, *Blackness and Race Mixture: The Dynamics of Racial Identity in
Columbia* [Baltimore, Md., 1993], 78). Obviously, not only Puerto Ricans of
African descent have wanted to distance themselves from their genealogy.

79. For a sensible attempt to understand the term *capitalism*, see Fernand

sees "the early development of a capitalist socioeconomic system in central Mexico."[80] His study of race and class in colonial Oaxaca, Mexico "can best be understood within the context of a developing system of commercial capitalism."[81] Anderson asked whether the economic and social stratification of Mexican society in 1821 should be seen "as . . . the result of economic changes accompanying the rise of early commercial capitalism,"[82] and he answered in the affirmative. Both Chance and Anderson are correct in their estimations of the nature of the economy. The Mexican economy, as well as other Spanish American economies, was one of commercial capitalism.[83] This does not mean that the colonial and early national economies had not advanced to varying degrees of maturity, for in fact there were differences between economies. What is important is that the Puerto Rican economy was also one of commercial capitalism, and this has fundamental implications.

The Puerto Rican economy was a market economy in which private property predominated and the profit motive prevailed. Imperial policy fixed many restrictions on the island's economy, some of which were liberalized during the last decades of the eighteenth century and then again in 1815, making possible the entrance into overseas trade of even modest entrepreneurs. The large majority of the free colored population operated at a much less elevated position in the economy; they were small farmers, artisans, street and market vendors, carters, domestics, and the like, occupations which, with the exception of the farmers, came under the purview of the town councils. These supervisory agencies greatly restricted the "free" functioning of the local marketplace. The nature of these restrictions was common among town councils throughout Span-

---

Braudel, *The Wheels of Commerce*, vol. 2 in *Civilization and Capitalism 15th–18th Century*, 3 vols., (tr.; New York, 1982–1984), 231–32.

80. Chance, *Race and Class in Colonial Oaxaca*, 197.

81. Ibid.

82. Anderson, "Race and Social Stratification," 212.

83. I have discussed the colonial economy and Marx's interpretation of capitalism more fully in *Independence in Spanish America: Civil Wars, Revolutions, and Underdevelopment* (Albuquerque, N.M., 1994), chapter 1.

ish America—Anglo-America also for that matter—and reflective of the councils' primary responsibility to maintain peace and order and ensure the availability of reasonably priced food.[84] The town councils were also charged with granting a variety of operating licenses and with supervising small retail stores, including those of the artisans, regarding weights and measures, general business practices, what might be sold or not sold, hours, prices, and so on. Additionally, they were the immediate supervisory agencies for the artisan guilds, controlling such matters as the nature of membership, testing, certification of master craftsmen, and election of officers. Thus, the "invisible hand of the marketplace" was encumbered in many instances, but it is important to bear in mind that precisely the same kinds of restrictions and governmental intervention existed in the United States, England, and in many other capitalist countries.

What does this mean for a study about racial prejudice? It means that Puerto Rico's free people of color possessed access to a market economy. It is extremely important to note that all business activities in colonial Spanish America functioned on the basis of contracts freely entered into, although there were several restrictions. With regard to free people of color in Puerto Rico, the most significant restrictions, other than those regarding age, were gender-related but color blind. If free people of color did not perform well in the economy, it was not because they were legally restricted from participating. The reason for such poor performance lies elsewhere.

In this matter, it is helpful to have a sense of what economic life was like for free people of color at the quotidian level, that is, the daily routine of ordinary life. Three points are salient: (1) the free people of color (as we shall see in the following chapter) could live wherever they wanted to in the city of San Juan; (2) so far as the law was concerned, free people of color could enter most occupations,

84. Standard treatments of the town councils are Constantino Bayle, *Los cabildos seculares en la América Española* (Madrid, 1952); John Preston Moore, *The Cabildo in Peru under the Hapsburgs* (Durham, N.C., 1954), and *The Cabildo in Peru under the Bourbons* (Durham, N.C., 1966).

including all crafts and all businesses;[85] and (3) during the first decades of the nineteenth century, the small port city of San Juan was not an entrepôt of dynamic economic activity and opportunity.[86] This means that it was difficult to make a living in San Juan, especially for the many newcomers—the in-migrants. The people of color who came of age in the city and the many who migrated from rural areas had to compete in an economy that did not grow by leaps and bounds. The problem was exacerbated by the large in-migration of whites from Spain during the first decades of the nineteenth century, as well as by refugees from the wars of independence in other colonies such as Venezuela. Furthermore, San Juan was a fortified city, important in the scheme of imperial defense, with several thousand military personnel stationed in and around the city. When mustered out, some of the soldiers remained in San Juan and sought to establish themselves in the economy. As a group the newcomers tended to be white and industrious. Some of them managed to become artisans, some storekeepers (even with initial capital investments of only a hundred or so pesos), and some highly capitalized entrepreneurs. Thus, employment opportunities were created for some people of color (including slaves) in the crafts, stores, and residences of the newcomers, but this inflow of people, skills, and capital narrowed the curve of opportunity for the free colored, and it was not good news for some whites.

As anyone who has been to "Old San Juan" knows, it is possible to walk through it in a matter of minutes, at least downhill from the Casals Museum toward the Bay, and if the pace is brisk and the

85. This beneficent occupational environment was encouraged by a relatively small number of free colored males in San Juan, meaning less competition for white males in the economy, a circumstance to be discussed in chapter 4.

86. It is often said that the *Cédula de Gracias* of 1815 greatly stimulated the Puerto Rican economy. See for instance, Arturo Santana, "Puerto Rico in a Revolutionary World," in Arturo Morales Carrión, ed., *Puerto Rico: A Political and Cultural History* (New York, 1983), 51–78. For a more balanced view, see Matos, "Economy, Society, and Urban Life," 46–47. The data presented in my book suggest that San Juan did not experience a great economic expansion during the first decades after 1815.

sun not too high overhead. On the other hand, it is possible to linger through a small, narrow street, enjoying the sounds, sights, smells—and what often is a throng of people. At any time during the decades discussed in this book, the city contained perhaps a hundred small retail grocery stores (*pulperías*), many of them at corners, where people purchased comestibles and other items, and socialized. Only a few of the grocers were free people of color, but many of the customers were. There were several small inns and taverns, some of these owned by people of color, including women, and their customers often were free people of color. Free people of color, perhaps in the majority, operated *mondoguerías*, which specialized in a tripe stew particularly appealing to customers of color.[87] Free colored women were domestics, laundresses, street hawkers, and many other things. Dozens of different kinds of artisans worked in San Juan: silversmiths, blacksmiths, tailors, shoemakers, coopers, caulkers, leather workers, seamstresses, milliners, carpenters, masons, bakers, and so on. Many of the artisans were free people of color, and many had shops.

As slave cities went, San Juan was a place of intimate physical and social contact between whites and free people of color. At any time during the first half of the nineteenth century, there were nearly as many free people of color as there were whites in San Juan, and in the barrio of Santa Bárbara there were more. With slaves added, roughly as many people of color lived in the city as whites. (The soldiers and sailors stationed at San Juan would have skewed the proportion toward a white majority, though.) What this means is that whites and free people of color shopped in each other's stores, bought things from each other's artisans, and ate in each

87. The information about *mondoguerías* is from Matos, "Economy, Society and Urban Life," 246–47. Matos also provides other information about free people of color in the workforce (see especially, 246–48; 253–58; 318–19). He has repeated some material from his dissertation in "Street Vendors, Pedlars, Shop-Owners and Domestics: Some Aspects of Women's Economic Roles in Nineteenth-Century San Juan, Puerto Rico (1820–1870)," in Verene Shepherd, et al., eds., *Engendering History: Caribbean Women in Historical Perspective* (New York, 1995), 176–93.

other's taverns and sweet shops. At any given time on any business day there might have been hundreds of people on any street or two near the central plaza, perhaps on Luna or San Francisco Streets, and approximately half of them might have been free people of color. In the evenings and on Sundays there would have been hundreds, perhaps even thousands, of people strolling, watching, or milling about, half of them colored. In San Juan whites and free people of color did business with each other, ate with each other, lived with each other, and, of course, in some instances slept with each other.

This openness and physical fluidity produced two fundamental results. One was that free people of color had freedom to participate in the economy, but as argued throughout this book, racial prejudice and discrimination limited this opportunity and caused systemic structural defects that insinuated themselves into the social and economic fabric. Another was that the free people of color overwhelmingly bought into the system: they desired to assimilate into white society, placing a premium on whiteness (as shall be demonstrated shortly) and access to all of the social, economic, and political advantages that attended whiteness.

One final matter to consider with regard to the economy is the question of class. Did Puerto Rican commercial capitalism divide the free colored population into classes? The term "class" is very contentious.[88] According to standard usage of the term, which has its etiology in Marxist (and/or Weberian) logic, it was in fact the Puerto Rican caste system that did not permit commercial capitalism to work its sway and produce a mature class system. However, there is another way to conceptualize class that is simpler, more straightforward, freer of encumbering philosophical argu-

88. I have discussed this issue in *Independence in Spanish America*. For a fuller consideration of class, as well as other matters of social stratification, see Magnus Mörner, "Classes, Strata and Elites: The Social Historian's Dilemma," in Magnus Mörner and Thommy Svensson, eds., *Classes, Strata and Elites: Essays on Social Stratification in Nordic and Third World History* (Göteborg, Sweden, 1988), 3–50.

ment, and ultimately more helpful in trying to understand the nature of Puerto Rican society during the nineteenth century. It is the definition offered by the sociologist Andrew Billingsley in his 1968 book *Black Families in White America*.[89] To Billingsley, the Negro community in the United States was divided into three classes: upper, middle, and lower, with each containing subgroups. Billingsley uses family income as the index of social class, an eminently intelligent and prudent taxonomic logic. On the one hand, it provides an escape from the Marxist argument, and, on the other, it allows a categorization of Puerto Rican society that offers some idea of the nature of economic performance and social pretension. Thus, by grouping free people of color into social classes according to family income, we have a useful guide to socioeconomic achievement that does not contradict the essential Puerto Rican social reality—the caste system. In Puerto Rico, therefore, as in the United States, a hierarchy of social classes functioned within the caste system.[90]

Employing the family income index to social class, it may be concluded that the overwhelming majority of Puerto Rico's free colored population were members of the lower class, but in both rural and urban areas there was a substantial, but as yet undetermined, number in the middle and upper classes. For those in the latter two classes, the legal disabilities and the stigma of the caste system must have been all the more disconcerting.

89. Billingsley, *Black Families in White America* (pb.; New York, 1968), 6–10.

90. For the classic statement of this experience in the United States, see John Dollard, *Caste and Class in a Southern Town* (2d ed.; New York, 1949).

3. Residential Patterns and Dwelling Ownership in San Juan, 1823–1846

THE PURPOSE OF THIS CHAPTER is to infer economic performance among San Juan's free colored population by employing dwelling ownership as an index. The absence of dwelling ownership does not of itself indicate poor economic performance, since members of any group being investigated might have elected to place their capital in rural lands or in store inventories, for instance, rather than buildings. Ownership of dwellings, on the other hand, does indeed suggest economic achievement.

It is extremely difficult to ascertain the degree of real property ownership among free people of color in urban areas of Spanish America, because the real property censuses normally did not enumerate the race of the property's owner. In San Juan, the problem is exacerbated because the honorifics *don* and *doña* were used so indiscriminately by census enumerators that they serve as an unreliable guide to race. This was not necessarily an unhealthy development in San Juan, and may in fact be taken as a sign of comparatively liberal social and racial attitudes, but it was nevertheless a development that limits the value of a traditional and widely used method of determining race. A further problem is that nominal censuses in Spanish America normally did not record property values. Hence, although there have been fine studies of free people of color in Spanish America (as well as in Brazil and the British West Indies), only modest attention has been paid to the matter of real property ownership.[1]

---

1. There are fragmentary data on real property ownership by free people of color in Havana suggestive of considerable wealth. See Pedro Deschamps Cha-

RESIDENTIAL PATTERNS

An evaluation of dwelling ownership among free people of color should consider the degree to which these legally and socially disadvantaged people were free to reside where they chose—that is, the degree to which their purchase of dwellings might have been impeded by legal or de facto segregation. To explore this issue it is worthwhile to have a familiarity with the city in question.

San Juan was a small city, both physically and demographically. The capital of the colony and the seat of the royal bureaucracy supported a population of only 7,658 people in 1820.[2] The reliable Pedro Tomás de Córdova, secretary to the governor, calculated the resident population in 1824 to be 8,453.[3] For 1828, Córdova presents the figure of 9,453 residents, plus several thousand soldiers and sailors, for a total of 12,744.[4] During the early nineteenth century, scores of provincial towns throughout Spanish America held populations as large or larger than San Juan's.

Toward the end of the eighteenth century, San Juan was 682 meters in length and 430 meters in breadth.[5] Running east to west

peaux, *El negro en la economía Habanera del siglo XIX* (Havana, 1971), 65–71, 79–80, 96, 124, 143–46, 179, 183. Jerome S. Handler provides interesting data on house ownership among freedmen in Barbados, although based on an admittedly very small sample (*The Unappropriated People* [Baltimore, Md., 1974], 144–46). Property ownership among the free people of color (pardos) of Caracas was apparently widespread during the latter part of the colonial era. See Kathleen Waldron's comment in "A Social History of a Primate City: The Case of Caracas, 1750–1810" (Ph.D. diss., Indiana University, 1977), 79. Patricia Seed makes an interesting observation about the relationship between "the acquisition of property" and the "upward socioeconomic mobility" of mulattoes in Mexico City in 1753 ("Social Dimensions of Race: Mexico City, 1753," *HAHR* 62:4 (Nov. 1982), 569–606.

2. AGPR, Gobernadores, Censos y Riqueza, 1801–1820, caja 11.

3. Pedro Tomás de Córdova, *Memorias geográficas, históricas ... de Puerto Rico*, II, 307.

4. Córdova, II, 13, 24–25, 397.

5. Adolfo de Hostos, *Historia de San Juan: Ciudad Murada, 1521–1898* (San Juan, 1966), 61. For a general survey of the development of San Juan, see

were five main through streets (*calles*). Running north to south were also five main through streets. Pedro Tomás de Córdova remembered that the "streets are cast in a straight line, they are of the same width, divided into . . . blocks of little more than one hundred yards."[6] The individual streets created by the crisscrossing of the through streets were the *cuadras*—that is, the facing pairs of blocks, or in some instances, a simple blockface. The blocks themselves were called *manzanas*. In 1820, there were fifty-eight *cuadras* in San Juan,[7] and the capital comprised four barrios (or administrative units often referred to as *cuarteles*): San Juan, San Francisco, Santo Domingo, and Santa Bárbara. By 1859, the much less populated barrios of Ballajá, De la Marina, and Puerto de Tierra had been added.[8]

The four historical barrios that form the core of this study comprised roughly the area incorporated in what today is referred to as "Old San Juan" or simply "San Juan." To the southwest was the

Aníbal Sepúlveda-Rivera, *San Juan: Historia de su desarrollo urbano, 1508–1898* (San Juan, 1989).

6. Hostos, *Historia de San Juan*, 79. Actually, Córdova used the terms *cuadra* and *manzana* interchangeably, observing that the *calles* were divided into "cuadras o manzanas" (ibid.). See also the description by Andre Pierre Ledrú, *Viaje a la Isla de Puerto Rico en el año 1787* (tr; San Juan, 1971), 64.

7. This is my calculation from the real property census of San Juan for 1820 (AGPR, Gobernadores, San Juan, 1816–1820, caja 561). There is no single title for this census, which exists only in manuscript form. Each barrio has its own title and title page. Thus, the title for the barrio of San Juan is "Justiprecio de los Edificios existentes en el Barrio de S. Juan. Año de 1820." Santo Domingo is simply "Quartel de Santo Domingo," although a long descriptive title appears on the first page.

For examples of the use of the terminology of urban form, see David J. Robinson and Michael M. Swann, "Geographical Interpretations of the Hispanic-American Colonial City: A Case Study of Caracas in the Late Eighteenth Century," in Robert J. Tata, ed., *Latin America: Search for Geographical Explanations* (Chapel Hill, N.C., 1976), 1–15; and Swann, *Tierra Adentro*, 277.

8. I have based this information about the added barrios on AGPR, Gobernadores, leg. num. 123-A, pieza I, Padrón o estadística general de la riqueza urbana de la Capital—Año de 1859. Hostos states that by 1853 the barrios of San Sebastián, Puerta de Tierra, and La Puntilla had been added to the historical four (*Historia de San Juan*, 79).

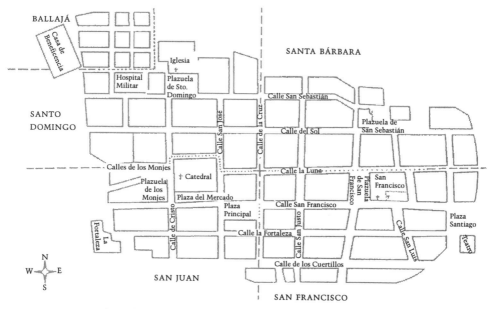

Map 2 Plan of the City of San Juan (ca. 1847–1853)

barrio of San Juan, the administrative and commercial center of the city. Here were to be found the offices of both the royal bureaucracy and the town council, as well as the city's main plaza and market. The Cathedral of San Juan was also located in this barrio of prestigious residence. As can be seen on the accompanying map, drawn from one from the period 1847–1853, the barrio of San Juan contained 11 *manzanas* and 22 *cuadras*.[9]

In the southeast part of the city and just to the east of the barrio of San Juan was the barrio of San Francisco. This barrio contained 17 *manzanas* and, depending on how one interprets the map of 1847–1853, between 27 and 32 *cuadras*. To the north of San Francisco was the barrio of Santa Bárbara, containing at midcentury 12 *manzanas* and between 24 and 27 *cuadras*. To the west of Santa Bárbara and north of San Juan lay the barrio of Santo Domingo,

9. The map is found in AGPR, Archivo Geográfico, caja/paquete 6, folio 355. The approximate date of the map was confirmed to me in a personal communication from Aníbal Sepúlveda-Rivera. See also María De Los Angeles Castro, *Arquitectura en San Juan de Puerto Rico (siglo XIX)* (Río Piedras, P.R., 1980), 134.

which contained 12 *manzanas* and between 25 and 29 *cuadras*. In addition to the important Dominican monastery, Santo Domingo housed the Military Hospital.

It is not possible to rank the four barrios in order of importance or prestige. The old view that the elite resided in or around the main plaza of colonial towns, although accurate in many instances, has been proven incorrect in others.[10] However, it is possible to gain some sense of their relative status in 1820 when a real property census was compiled.[11] In that year, the barrio of San Juan contained buildings and vacant lots (*solares*) with a combined value of 445,500 pesos (Table 3.1). Santo Domingo's buildings and lots were valued at 386,025 pesos. Santa Bárbara had the lowest gross valuation—290,570 pesos—and San Francisco the highest—774,300 pesos. Although San Francisco, with the greatest number of properties, had the highest gross valuation, it did not have the highest mean valuation. It was San Juan, just as one would expect of the administrative and commercial center of the city, that held, on average, the most valuable properties.

This was the case also when it came to privately owned dwellings (Table 3.2). San Juan, with the fewest dwellings, had overwhelmingly the highest mean valuation, whereas Santa Bárbara was the barrio where dwelling values were lowest.

The majority of the city's houses and lots in 1820 were modestly valued, ranging between 1,000 and 5,000 pesos. Nearly 200 properties were valued at less than 1,000 pesos (with only 36 vacant lots in the city), and more than 400 properties at less than 2,000 pesos. Santa Bárbara held the greatest number of very inexpensive properties.

Free people of color resided in all of the barrios, and in substan-

---

10. See Fred Bronner, "Urban Society in Colonial Spanish America: Research Trends," *LARR* 21:1 (1986), 7–72, 24–25; and Anderson, "Race and Social Stratification," 209–43.

11. See note 7. The census of 1820 did not include several important public and Church buildings—such as the cathedral, monasteries and convents. It did include vacant lots—*solares*. It appears that all Church-owned dwellings that were rented out were included. Valuations were either not given or were unknown in 14 instances.

Table 3.1. Property Valuations by Barrio in San Juan, 1820

N	Barrio	Sum (Pesos)	Mean (Pesos)
127	San Juan	445,500	3,507.9
158	Santo Domingo	386,025	2,443.2
194	Santa Bárbara	290,570	1,497.8
317	San Francisco	774,300	2,442.6
796	The City	1,896,395	2,382.4

Source: AGPR, Gobernadores, San Juan, 1816–1820, caja 561: real property census of San Juan.

Table 3.2. Valuations of Privately Owned Dwellings by Barrio
in San Juan, 1820

N	Barrio	Sum (Pesos)	Mean (Pesos)
126	San Juan	443,000	3,515.9
149	Santo Domingo	346,500	2,325.5
169	Santa Bárbara	277,220	1,640.4
304	San Francisco	764,450	2,514.6
748	The City	1,831,170	2,448.1

Source: Same as Table 3.1.

tial numbers. In 1823, approximately 59 percent of the free population of the barrio of Santa Bárbara were free colored. In 1828, in the barrio of San Juan, almost certainly the most prestigious barrio, approximately 38 percent of those who were free were people of color. In the barrio with the greatest number of dwellings in 1820, San Francisco, approximately 38 percent of the free population in 1833 were colored. Some 43 percent of the free population of the first *trozo* of Santo Domingo were colored in 1846.

Not only did free people of color reside in each of the four barrios, but they also resided on every street in the barrios of Santa Bárbara and Santo Domingo (first *trozo*), and on every block (and perhaps street) in the barrios of San Juan and San Francisco. The census of the barrio of Santa Bárbara for 1823 does not group houses according to blocks or streets, so the following discussion considers only the barrios of San Juan, San Francisco, and Santo Domingo. A nominal census of the barrio of Santa Bárbara for 1818, however, makes it clear that free people of color also lived on each of that barrio's streets.[12]

Although whites and free people of color were separated by law in many ways, they were clearly willing to live side by side with each other.[13] Table 3.3 contains the number of white and free colored heads of households (coresident families, including solitar-

12. AGPR, Gobernadores, Municipales, San Juan, 1816–1820, caja 561, Padrón de los vecinos del Cuartel de Santa Bárbara. Año de 1818. A quite different residential pattern prevailed in the urban centers of Jalapa and Orizaba, Mexico during the late eighteenth century (Patrick J. Carroll, *Blacks in Colonial Veracruz: Race, Ethnicity, and Regional Development* [Austin, Tex., 1991], 115.

13. Degler makes the interesting point that in Brazil the racial system, which recognized many categories of racial mixture, "makes most difficult, if not impossible, the kind of segregation patterns that have been so characteristic of the United States. With many shades of skin color, segregating people on the basis of color would incur both enormous expense and great inconvenience.... Furthermore ... families would be split by the color line" (*Neither Black nor White*, 224). This has a nice practical ring to it, but I suspect that other factors are far more consequential in determining patterns of Brazilian segregation or lack of it. In Puerto Rico, which also recognized categories of racial mixture, segregation was, I believe, a strong possibility. Puerto Rico had no problem segregating people of color as with legal disabilities, the segregated militia, or such grotesque rulings as Governor Prim's attack on the African race. On the other hand, after the so-called "Conspiracy of La Escalera" in 1844, Cuba reversed its policy of dividing the free people of color into different racial categories and began to combine them into one racial group. Simultaneously, the Cuban government began to increase the restrictions placed upon the free people of color (see Robert L. Paquette, *Sugar Is Made with Blood: The Conspiracy of La Escalera and the Conflict between Empires over Slavery in Cuba* [Middletown, Conn., 1988], 104–28). Presumably, the new racial policies were linked, but there is no reason to believe that the government could not have increased restrictions on the free people of color without categorizing them as a single racial entity. It is worth noting, however, that in either case the free people of lightest skin color generally must have felt the greatest indignation.

Table 3.3. White and Free Colored Heads of Households Resident in the
Barrios of San Juan (1828), San Francisco (1833), and Santo Domingo (1846)

						San Juan (1828)					
Block	1	2	3	4	5	6	7	8	9	10	
White	51	15	27	20	31	31	31	22	12	5	
Free Colored	20	4	12	9	19	25	17	32	9	1	

						San Francisco (1833)					
Block	1	4	5	6	10	11	12	13	14	15	17
White	72	23	33	15	40	32	19	16	24	8	103
Free Colored	48	16	19	26	31	30	10	23	14	1	61

				Santo Domingo (1846)			
Street	1	2	3	4	5	6	7
White	21	28	42	32	43	16	1
Free Colored	11	19	25	17	41	14	2

Note: The censuses for the barrios of San Juan and San Francisco used the term *manzana,* which meant block. (Block 10 is actually the Real Parque de Artillería.) The census for Santo Domingo used the word *calle* (street) as did the nominal census of the barrio of Santa Bárbara for 1818, mentioned above. For the barrio of Santo Domingo, the numbered streets in the table refer, in order, to: Cruz, Luna, San José, San Sebastián, Sol, and Cristo.

The few *agregado* families are not included in this Table or in Table 3.4. For a discussion of *agregados,* see note 31.

ies—be they single, married or widowed) resident on each block in the barrios of San Juan and San Francisco and on each street in the first *trozo* of Santo Domingo. By any useful definition, this was an unsegregated city.[14] On several of the blocks, whites and free people

14. It is of some interest that a study of Puerto Rican racial attitudes at mid-twentieth century reported an extremely high degree of residential segregation by whites of the upper classes in certain areas of greater San Juan (Eduardo Seda Bonilla, "Dos modelos de relaciones raciales," *Mundo Nuevo* 3:31 [Jan. 1969], 38). No valid comparison can be made to the absence of segregation in the four historical barrios between 1823 and 1846, since in the modern period many Puerto Ricans who would have been categorized as free colored were now considered white.

of color resided in almost perfect parity. On only one, block number 6 in San Francisco in 1833, were there more free colored than white heads of households.

This apparently liberal attitude toward residential selection on the part of whites and free people of color meant that no area of the barrios studied was overwhelmingly free colored, and thus likely to have been shunned by white storekeepers to the advantage of free colored entrepreneurs. One of the consequences of residential segregation in other parts of the Americas is that colored storekeepers and professionals sometimes have found themselves with freedom from white competition and with virtually a captive market. After studying fifteen cities in both the North and South of the United States during the first half of the nineteenth century, Leonard P. Curry concluded that "north of the slave states, the development of black entrepreneurial activity seems to be directly related to the degree of residential segregation."[15] Boston, the most heavily segregated of the cities Curry studied, had the second greatest percentage of blacks involved in entrepreneurial endeavors, exceeded only by New Orleans, which was also heavily segregated.[16] Although there is no systematic study of entrepreneurial activity at the lower reaches of the economic continuum in this period of Puerto Rican history, my own work on the small retail grocers—the *pulperos*—in San Juan suggests at most very few free people of color among them.[17] It would be ironic if a seemingly liberal attitude toward integration of the races unintentionally contributed to limited economic opportunity among San Juan's free colored population.

Although an extreme example of an unsegregated city, San Juan was not unique in Spanish America. Dennis Valdes found that "racial and class segregation by zones or blocks . . . did not occur in eighteenth-century Mexico City."[18] Studying the "southwest cuar-

15. Leonard P. Curry, *The Free Black in Urban America, 1800–1850: The Shadow of the Dream* (Chicago, 1981), 24.

16. Ibid. and p. 56.

17. Jay Kinsbruner, "The Pulperos of Caracas and San Juan during the First Half of the Nineteenth Century," *LARR* 13:1 (1978), 65–85.

18. Valdes, "The Decline of the *Sociedad de Castas*," 114.

tel of the Spanish sector" of Mexico City in 1753, Valdes calculated that *pardo* (here a general term for free colored) heads of households resided on 29 of the cuartel's 36 streets.[19] Anderson has observed that in Guadalajara, Mexico, in 1821 "not only did non-don Spaniards live in the same cuartel with Indians and castas, but they often lived side by side in the same block or rubbed elbows within the same household."[20] Chance has shown that in 1792 there was some clustering by peninsular Spaniards (born in Spain) in Oaxaca, but that all other groups, including mulattoes, lived throughout the city according to no pattern of segregation.[21]

However, the absence of residential segregation does not mean the absence of a caste system. Chance studied segregation in Oaxaca within a hypothesis drawn "from the ecological branch of urban sociology," which, in his words, posits "a general fit between residential distribution of race and class on the one hand, and the place of these dimensions within the overall urban social structure on the other."[22] It may be that Chance is correct in his conclusion about caste and class in Oaxaca, but his sociological hypothesis is invalid in the case of San Juan, where residential integration cannot be taken as proof of the decline of the caste system and its replacement by a class system. In San Juan, the caste system continued to prevail, even as commercial capitalism attenuated its harshness and challenged its fundamental principles. Racial prejudice in Puerto Rico was complex, its cosmology the result of many factors. It was a racial prejudice that could support many tradi-

19. Ibid., 136–37.

20. Anderson, "Race and Social Stratification," 230. It should be noted that Guadalajara contained only a "small scattering" of free people of color (215).

21. John K. Chance, "The Ecology of Race and Class in Late Colonial Oaxaca," in David J. Robinson, ed., *Studies in Spanish American Population History* (Boulder, Colo., 1981), 93–117. Chance used a Segregation Index that considers several racial groups; thus, his figures are not compatible with mine.

22. Chance, "Ecology of Race and Class," 96. For examples of other variables in conjunction with place of residence, see Valdes, "The Decline of the *Sociedad de Castas*," 114–35, and Anderson, "Race and Social Stratification," 228.

tional Spanish strictures against full participation of the free people of color and simultaneously allow residential integration.

That the San Juan areas studied were virtually integrated becomes more apparent when the city is compared with others using a statistic known as the Segregation Index, which is an index of dissimilarity. Although it is both a crude and controversial measure of segregation, employed cautiously it is useful for comparative purposes. Simply put, the Segregation Index measures the percentage of whites and nonwhites who would have to be moved from one geographical unit, in this case block or street, to another in order to produce a racial proportion roughly equal to that of the city or barrio at large.[23]

The values expressed by the Segregation Index range from 0 to 100, with the lower values representing less segregation and the higher values greater segregation. For the barrio of San Juan in 1828, the Segregation Index of heads of households was 15.9; for the barrio of San Francisco in 1833, it was 12.7; and for the first *trozo* of the barrio of Santo Domingo in 1846, it was 13.0. The Segregation Index at the block or street level may be seen in Table 3.4. Clearly, the total impression is one of little, if any, segregation. (For a fuller discussion of the Segregation Index, see Appendix B).

The Segregation Index may be used for comparison with United States cities, for which extensive data are available on the spatial distribution of white and black residents. Working with individuals

23. For the Segregation Index, I followed Karl E. Taeuber and Alma F. Taeuber, *Negroes in Cities: Residential Segregation and Neighborhood Change* (New York, 1969), 28–35, 236–37, and *passim*. See also Curry, *The Free Black*, 54–55. The Index is calculated as Segregation Index=½ (sum $N_i/N - W_i/W$) where N_i=nonwhite at block or street level; N=nonwhite at barrio level; W_i=white at block or street level; W=white at barrio level.

One limitation of the Segregation Index is that it unrealistically presumes that factors such as income or cultural achievement, for instance, are not influential in residential selection. A further problem is that not all censuses measure at the same geographical level, thus limiting the usefulness of the Index for comparative purposes. Yet, the values for three of San Juan's barrios are so consistent and so different from what one might have expected of a slave society that they are indeed useful.

Table 3.4. Indices of Residential Segregation for Three San Juan Barrios,
1828–1846

San Juan (1828)										
Block	1	2	3	4	5	6	7	8	9	10
SI	3.25	1.59	1.24	0.88	0.34	2.37	0.34	4.54	0.69	0.65
San Francisco (1833)										
Block	1	4	5	6	10	11	12	13		
SI	0.75	0.12	0.88	2.71	0.36	1.22	0.68	2.04		
Street	14	15	17							
SI	0.61	0.86	2.45							
Santo Domingo (1846)										
Block	1	2	3	4	5	6	7			
SI	1.19	1.12	1.95	2.26	5.10	0.86	0.56			

Note: SI = Segregation Index. The block numbers for San Francisco follow the census.

and wards rather than households and blocks or streets, Curry has calculated Segregation Indices for 15 cities in the United States between 1820 and 1850.[24] In 4 decennial years beginning with 1820, Boston's Index ran between 46.3 and 59.2. In 1820, the Index for New Orleans was 11.6, but by 1850 it had risen to 45.2. Charleston's had increased from 10.0 in 1830 to 20.6 in 1850. Baltimore's was relatively low: 13.1 in 1820, 11.6 in 1830, 9.9 in 1840, and 21.5 in 1850.[25] Working with households and blocks, the Taeubers have computed Segregation Indices for 109 cities in the United States for 1940, 1950, and 1960. In almost every instance, the values were either in the 70s, 80s, or 90s. New Orleans', for instance, ranged between 81.0 and 86.3. Baltimore's ran from 90.1 to 89.6. Among the 45 southern cities analyzed, Charleston's were always the lowest values, ranging from 60.1 to 79.5.[26] The magnitude of these

24. Curry, *The Free Black,* 56.
25. Ibid. I have rounded Curry's numbers to tenths.
26. Taeuber and Taeuber, *Negroes in Cities,* 39–41.

Indices for the modern period places San Juan's low nineteenth-century values in sharp relief.

Nowhere was the general absence of residential segregation in San Juan more apparent than at the level of individual houses. In San Juan, whites frequently lived next door to free people of color, and, more interestingly, often resided within the same buildings, just as they did in the Mexico City cuartel of 1753 studied by Valdes.[27] During the first half of the nineteenth century, there were three types of buildings in the city of San Juan. Most prevalent were *casas*—that is, houses. There were also a few *bohíos*, generally thatch-roofed shacks.[28] The third type of edifice was the nonprivate building—public, Church, or military—in which a few people lived. In this discussion, the term "house" includes *casas* and *bohíos*.

The degree to which whites and free people of color shared houses in the city of San Juan is impressive. There were 205 occupied houses in the barrio of Santa Bárbara in 1823, and in 78 of them (38.0 percent) resided both white and free colored families, including solitaries. More remarkably, perhaps, in the barrio of San Juan in 1828 there were 131 occupied houses, and the races were mixed in 83 of them (63.4 percent). Similarly, in the barrio of San Francisco in 1833 there were 275 occupied houses, and families of different races resided in 164 (60.0 percent). By a slight majority, commingling of the races also prevailed in the first *trozo* of the barrio of Santo Domingo in 1846, where there were 128 occupied houses, with families of different races residing in 63 of them (49.2 percent).[29]

27. Valdes, "The Decline of the *Sociedad de Castas*," 114–35.

28. The barrio of Santa Bárbara contained 31 *bohíos* in 1823, but in that year the governor took steps to prohibit the future building of such shacks, and the town council soon ordered that all *bohíos* within the city's walls be destroyed (Hostos, *Historia de San Juan*, 78). These efforts seem to have been effective, since there were no *bohíos* in the barrio of San Juan in 1828, only one in the barrio of San Francisco in 1833, and none in the first *trozo* of the barrio of Santo Domingo in 1846. The number of *bohíos* is from the census of the barrio of Santa Bárbara for 1823.

29. For all houses, the mean number of occupants per building was 5.7 for the barrio of Santa Bárbara; 8.9 for the barrio of San Juan; 6.9 for the barrio of San Francisco; and 6.9 for the first *trozo* of the barrio of Santo Domingo.

The several hundred examples of houses with both white and free colored families resident are of interest for what they reveal about race relations in the slave city of San Juan. In the barrio of San Francisco in 1833, for instance, a town councilman, Don José Izquirdo, who owned and lived in his own house, rented rooms or apartments to several free colored households. In another instance, a white family rented an apartment from a free colored owner who resided in the building. Other similar cases can easily be cited. However, to pursue this dimension of the free colored experience, the barrio of San Juan will be singled out for discussion. It is precisely there, the seat of local and royal government and the center of business activity, that one might expect to find a harsh separation of the races, not the reverse.

Many houses in the city of San Juan were extremely large, some housing 30, 40, or 50 people. Often they resembled boarding houses, and perhaps some were just that, although the censuses are silent on the matter. In some instances, this "boarding house effect" may have contributed to an intermingling of the races. For instance, 37 people lived in house number 2 located on block 1 of the barrio of San Juan in 1828. The house was owned by the estate of the late Don José Ribera and in 1820 was valued at 6,000 pesos. Ribera's estate now rented or otherwise provided the house to Don Manuel Aldea, a 31-year-old white man married to Ribera's 52-year-old widow. Aldea, or the estate, in turn rented out seven apartments. The first renting head of household was white, the second free colored, and the third white. The rest of the renters were all free colored. House number 5 on the same block held 40 people and was rented by Don Juan de Dios Cuevas, a Spanish bureaucrat. Cuevas provided apartments to 3 renters, one an 80-year-old free colored widow. House number 27 on block 3 was valued at a substantial 9,000 pesos in 1820. The owners, three siblings, lived in the house but rented it to Don Francisco Gonsález de Linares, a 50-year-old Spaniard who resided there with his family. It was he who apparently rented apartments to 7 others, among whom were 2 free people of color and their families. Together, 52 people lived in the building. House number 86 on block 6 also seems to have had the quality of a boarding house. Thirty-nine people lived in it. At its head was Doña Josefa Montenegro, the 40-year-old white widow of the dwelling's owner. Doña Josefa rented apartments to 13 heads of separate households, 5 white and 8 free colored. Clearly, not only were some San Juan houses large and densely populated, they were highly integrated.

Other housing arrangements are especially suggestive. House number 12 on block 1 was rented by Don Mariano Taforo, a white military officer from Spain, who resided with his family. The owner of the house, also resident, was a free colored widow who lived there with her daughter and three slaves. Just a short distance away, in house 13, lived the intendant, Don Mariano Sixto from Madrid, the colony's second ranking royal official. It appears, but it is not certain, that Sixto rented the house and, in turn, rented apartments to four other people. The first three renters were white, but the fourth was free colored. If the intendant lived in a house occupied also by free people of color, it is not surprising that the practice would be commonplace.

Churchmen could also be unbiased in their attitudes toward housing arrangements. House number 42 on block 3 was owned by the Presbyter Don José Marcos Santaella and rented to José Morales, who worked at the *presideo*. Morales was a 60-year-old white widower from Spain who lived with his four free colored children and one free colored grandchild. House number 44 on the same block was owned by the Presbyter Don José Mateos Santaella. Santaella was a 63-year-old white cleric from Spain who lived in this house with a 44-year-old single free colored woman (his guest) and 2 slaves. He also rented 3 apartments to free people of color. Interestingly, house number 45 was owned by Dr. Don Francisco Marcos Santaella, a 54-year-old white fiscal of the royal treasury, who lived there with his wife, 8 children, 2 guests, and 7 slaves. Although living on the same block as the other Santaellas, Don Francisco was from Puerto Rico, and one can only wonder whether the 3 men were related. This one rented 3 apartments to whites and 1 to a free person of color. House number 49 on block 3 was owned by the Church's tax office. In it 8 apartments were rented, 3 by whites and 5 by free people of color.

It is in the context of such manifest freedom of residential choice that one can fully appreciate the nature of house ownership among San Juan's free people of color—both the degree to which they owned dwellings, and equally important, the degree to which they did not.

HOUSE OWNERSHIP

San Juan was a city of renters. Very few free people of color or whites owned houses, nor were there enough structures for many to have done so.[30] However, a much higher percentage of white heads of households owned their own houses than did free people of color.[31] Only in Santa Bárbara, the barrio with by far the lowest mean value of dwellings in 1820, was the percentage of ownership among heads of households fairly close between free people of color and whites (see Table 3.5). In 1823, the barrio of Santa Bárbara clearly was a place of real property ownership opportunity for free people of color, but the data suggest a specific relationship between such opportunity and modest property values. Certainly, very few free colored heads of households were capable of purchasing a dwelling in the other barrios.

This is not the entire story of house ownership among free people of color, however. If the data are refined to exclude those heads of households who were not also the heads of the Residential Units (RUs), a somewhat different picture emerges. The heads of Residen-

30. For a discussion of the transition from the earlier single household in Spanish America to multiple household residential structures and of the increase in rental housing units, see Robinson and Swann, "Geographical Interpretations," 1–15, and Swann, *Tierra Adentro*, 283–85.

31. There was also a group of people enumerated in the censuses as *agregados*. Scholars have characterized urban *agregados* variously as boarders, guests, or unpaid domestics. Although there sometimes were families among the *agregados* in the four San Juan barrios, in my definition they did not form separate households (and thus are not included in the tables and figures). In the city of San Juan, *agregados* were relatives, guests, boarders, and, it seems safe to conclude, domestics, whether remunerated with wages or not. I believe we must consider some of the San Juan *agregados* as transients, and to a greater degree than the general population.

Table 3.5. Percent of House Ownership by White and Free Colored Heads
of Households by Barrio in San Juan, 1823–1846

	White		Free Colored	
Santa Bárbara	14.3%*	13.6%†	14.0%*	13.4%†
San Juan	12.2	11.8	1.2	1.2
San Francisco	15.8	14.4	2.4	2.2
Santo Domingo (1st *trozo*)	8.7	8.0	1.4	1.3

*Coded conventionally.
†Coded alternatively (see Appendix B).

tial Units were those heads of households (including solitaries) who
were the owners or primary renters of the houses they lived in, and
who, if theirs were multiple residences, rented one or more apartments (or rooms) to other households. In this usage, the term *Residential Unit* follows the Joint Oxford-Syracuse Project and simply
means a dwelling with "any number of households."[32] It is further
assumed that one household "serves as the main household."[33]

32. Linda L. Greenow, "Spatial Dimensions of Household and Family in
Eighteenth-Century Spanish America" (discussion paper no. 35, Department of
Geography, Syracuse University, 1977), 10. That it is extremely difficult to
standardize terminology may be seen in Greenow's discussion of the literature
in "Family, Household and Home: A Micro-Geographic Analysis of Cartagena
(New Granada) in 1777" (discussion paper no. 18, Department of Geography,
Syracuse University, 1976), 17.

33. Greenow, "Spatial Dimensions," 10. However, in the case of the city of
San Juan, it is not always possible to determine which household was the main
household. When several households rented within one Residential Unit, and
the first household listed in the census manifested no decidedly superior economic status, it is unwise to hold that the first one listed was the main household. In fact, the several households might have rented independently, with no
family enjoying a superior position vis-á-vis the others. If the first listed household owned the house, I have assumed that it was the main household since it
rented to others, but there are also instances when the household that owned
the structure or the part of the structure serving as a residence was not the first
one listed in the Residential Unit. In those instances, I normally assumed that
the first listed household was the main household under the presumption that
it rented the house from the owner and, in turn, rented space to additional

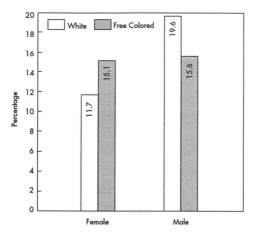

Figure 3.1. House Ownership by Heads of Residential Units, by Race and Sex, Santa Bárbara, 1823

Being the head of a Residential Unit frequently implied some degree of achievement and responsibility beyond what normally would be associated with simple tenancy. The head of a Residential Unit who rented to other households was, after all, a landlord. Thus, when only this group is considered, the degree of house ownership among free people of color becomes both more impressive and somewhat provocative.

As one would expect, there existed a substantial degree of house ownership among free colored heads of Residential Units in the barrio of Santa Bárbara in 1823. In addition, approximately the same degree of house ownership prevailed among both male and female free colored heads of Residential Units, whereas in the case of whites there existed a greater degree of ownership among males than among females (see Figure 3.1). The degree of house ownership

households (including that of the owner, through whatever arrangement). There are, however, some instances when it is not at all clear from the census that the first listed household was in any way in a position superior to the others. In such cases, the house was considered to have had no head of the Residential Unit, with the result that the number of heads of Residential Units in Figures 3.1–3.3 is less than the number of houses in each barrio.

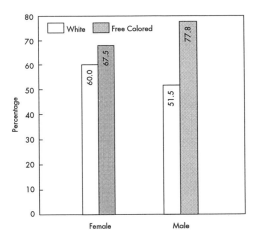

Figure 3.2. House Ownership by Heads of Residential Units, within Each Race and Sex, Santa Bárbara, 1823

by free people of color is impressive with respect to that of the whites of both sexes, but it is no doubt significant that white males displayed the highest degree of ownership, an indication of their ability to be the basic family provider.

It is also of interest that a greater percentage of free colored female and male heads of Residential Units owned the houses in which they lived than their white female and male counterparts (Figure 3.2). This is not what one would have expected. It means that among those free colored men and women who were successful enough in the economy and who exerted enough initiative to become or remain heads of Residential Units, there was an even greater degree of residential ownership and, in this regard, achievement than among whites. To be sure, this fairly widespread dwelling ownership occurred in the barrio of Santa Bárbara, where housing was the cheapest in the city in 1820 and more than likely for a long while thereafter. That more free colored female heads of Residential Units owned the dwellings in which they lived than did their white female counterparts may in part have been the consequence of lower marital rates among the free colored women, a reflection of severe demographic problems within the free colored community, a point which shall be discussed in chapter 4.

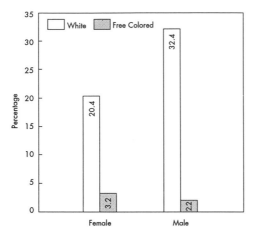

Figure 3.3. House Ownership by Heads of Residential Units, by Race and Sex, San Juan, 1828

Few free colored heads of Residential Units owned the houses in which they lived in the other barrios (Figures 3.3, 3.4, and 3.5). When compared with the degree of house ownership among whites, the degree of ownership among the free colored was generally miniscule in the barrios of San Juan, San Francisco, and Santo Domingo. In each instance it was also less than occurred among free colored heads of Residential Units in the barrio of Santa Bárbara.[34] Among whites, the number of heads of Residential Units who owned dwellings in the three barrios and (to a lesser extent) the first *trozo* of Santo Domingo[35] is more substantial, and, in each

34. In Durango, New Spain, in 1778, 12.5 percent of Residential Units were owned by nonwhites, "and most of these [resident] household heads were mulattos" (Swann, *Tierra Adentro*, 301). Matos has provided information about Residential Units for three of the San Juan barrios for 1833 and 1846, but because of coding differences his data are not compatible with mine. See Matos, "Economy, Society and Urban Life," 137–39.

35. That so few white and free colored heads of Residential Units owned their dwellings in the first *trozo* of the barrio of Santo Domingo in 1846 is difficult to explain without knowing the value of housing at that late date. There is a real property census for the municipality of San Juan in 1859, which lists property values, but it is not divided into barrios (AGPR, Gobernadores, Municipales, año de 1859, leg. 123-A, pieza I).

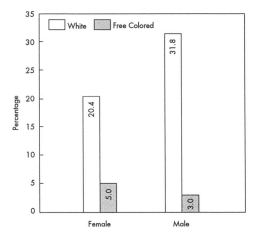

Figure 3.4. House Ownership by Heads of Residential Units, by Race and Sex, San Francisco, 1833

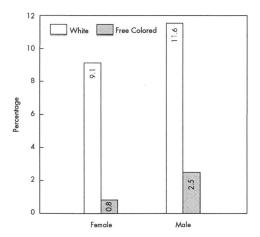

Figure 3.5. House Ownership by Heads of Residential Units, by Race and Sex, Santo Domingo (first *trozo*), 1846

instance, more white males than females were represented. The pattern appears indicative of a healthy demographic and economic performance among whites, and, more generally, of a white dominant society.

Notwithstanding the imbalance in ownership, those free people of color who owned houses were sometimes an impressive group who belie their standard characterization. Perhaps the most famous description of housing in the city of San Juan during the colonial period was made by Fray Iñigo Abbad y Lasierra in 1782. Abbad recorded that the Spaniards and well-to-do residents lived in houses made of stone and covered by tiles. Some had flat brick roofs. The houses of the mulattoes and people of color were made of wood. Those of the blacks and poor people were coarser and smaller, little more than straw cages, supported by canes and covered by palm leaves. These were the *bohíos*.[36] By the 1820s, however, the picture was somewhat different. Abbad certainly did not include free people of color among the well-to-do residents, but, in the early decades of the nineteenth century, some of them owned stone dwellings, and some even owned the generally more valuable two-story buildings.

Several examples from the barrio of Santa Bárbara serve to illustrate that free people of color were not limited to the ownership of inexpensive houses. In 1820, when the mean value of a privately owned edifice in the barrio was 1,640 pesos, one 40-year-old free colored resident had inherited a house valued at 3,000 pesos.[37] Bartolomé Cueto, a 40-year-old free colored, owned a house with an estimated value of 2,500 pesos. At 43, Antonio Arriago, free colored, owned three houses, apparently contiguous, with values of 1,500, 3,000, and 2,000 pesos. Don Atlántico Vargas was a 50-year-old free colored grocer—a *pulpero*. In 1820, he owned a house valued at 2,000 pesos. A man of the same name, almost certainly the same person, owned a house on the same street valued at 2,100

36. Abbad y Lasierra, *Historia geográfica, civil y política . . . de Puerto Rico,* 94–95. Abbad's description is repeated in Aníbal Sepúlveda-Rivera, "San Juan de Puerto Rico: Growth of a Caribbean Capital City" (Ph.D. diss., Cornell University, 1986), 174. I have both translated Abbad and used parts of Sepúlveda-Rivera's translation. See also the description of San Juan in 1797 in Ledrú, *Viaje a la isla de Puerto Rico,* 95, and Sepúlveda-Rivera, "San Juan de Puerto Rico," 175–76.

37. The data in the first part of this paragraph are derived from the following documents: AGPR, Gobernadores, San Juan, Municipales, 1816–1820, real property census of 1820 and caja 561, Padrón de . . . Santa Bárbara: Año 1818.

pesos. Among free colored women who owned property was Rita Molina, 40, whose house was valued at 1,800 pesos.

The property ownership of some free people of color suggests their considerable economic success. In 1845, Manuel Elías, a free colored silversmith, owned the three contiguous two-story houses, on Calle San Francisco in the barrio of that name, which he had inherited from his father, Pedro Elías.[38] In 1820, when still owned by the father, the houses were valued at 3,500, 3,000, and 1,500 pesos respectively.[39] In 1833, Manuel, along with his wife, five children, and three slaves lived in house number 154; he rented out houses 155 and 156. In 1845, Elías not only owned the three houses on Calle San Francisco, but a fourth on Calle del Sol.[40] In 1847, Antonio Cruzado inherited a house from a former slave. He quickly sold the house for 2,300 pesos.[41] A month later, he also sold, for 3,350 pesos, a one-story stone house which he had built at his own expense on a lot he purchased in 1841.[42] In 1854, he sold another one-story stone house, this one for 2,150 pesos.[43] Yet, in 1854 he still owned one more stone house of the same type.[44]

The accomplishments of some free people of color are all the more impressive when one considers their inauspicious beginnings, as in the case of Antonio Cruzado's benefactor, the former slave María Francisca Ferrer. She and her husband, both born

38. AGPR, PN, San Juan, caja 437, will of Manuel Elías, October 12, 1845, fols. 478–90v. See also Elías's father's will, caja 527, April 7, 1824, fols. 279–81.

39. Property census of San Juan for 1820, AGPR, Gobernadores, San Juan 1816–1820, caja 561.

40. AGPR, PN, caja 437, fols. 478–80v.

41. Ibid., caja 439, record of sale, Cruzado to González, June 22, 1847, fols. 422v–25v.

42. Ibid., caja 439, record of sale, Cruzado to Ezguiaga, July 28, 1847, fols. 518–522. He also owned another single-storied stone house on Calle la Luna, this one purchased in 1847 for 1,825 pesos (ibid., caja 530, record of sale, Pozo to Cruzado, September 10, 1847, fols. 200–200v and 204–205).

43. Ibid., caja 261, record of sale, Cruzado to Cabrera, February 4, 1854, fols. 52–54.

44. Ibid., caja 261, notice of sales tax payment, December 7, 1854, fols. 623–27.

in Africa, were *libertos* when they wrote their joint will in 1846. They were legitimately married, and they had six children, but all died in infancy. During their marriage the pair acquired and lived in a single-storied, stone house on Calle San Justo (probably in the barrio of San Francisco). They owned two male slaves. It appears that the husband was a carpenter. At any rate, the pair had acquired some wealth. They left 50 pesos for the celebration of a fiesta. They left money for the establishment of chaplancies, one for 250 pesos. Another 125 pesos they left for the saying of mass. The husband had a son out of wedlock, and to him he left 500 pesos. Altogether, this was an impressive amount of money saved by two former slaves.[45] The following year, the wife, now a widow, wrote her own will. She repeated basically the same religious bequests made the previous year. To two godsons she left all of the carpentry tools in her possession. She owed her deceased husband's natural son 232 pesos, the amount remaining of his inheritance. Her executor and heir was Antonio Cruzado.[46] Thus, Antonio Cruzado, free colored, was given a helpful boost in life.

As we have seen, women were often owners of dwellings. In March 1841, Rosa Peña, free colored, after requesting and receiving permission from her husband (as any married woman would have had to do in what was still a Spanish colony), sold a one-story stone house at the Plazuela Santiago, in the barrio of San Francisco, for 1,700 pesos. She had bought it in 1832 for 550 pesos.[47] The following month, Peña purchased a single-storied stone house on Sol for 1,600 pesos.[48] In 1844, again with permission from her husband, Peña sold this new house for a handsome 3,500 pesos.[49]

45. Ibid., caja 438, will of Joaquín Cruz and María Francisca Ferrer, March 16, 1846, fols. 156–57v.

46. Ibid., caja 439, will of María Francisca Ferrer, March 9, 1847, fols. 169–70v.

47. Ibid., caja 528, record of sale, Peña to Mediavilla, March 4, 1841, fols. 90–93 (the second half of the volume); caja 480, record of sale, Latorre to Peña, March 23, 1832, fols. 178v–83v.

48. Ibid., caja 528, record of sale, Cambián to Peña, April 29, 1841, fols. 166v–69.

49. Ibid., caja 530 (Tomo 1859), record of sale, Peña to Ortiz de Zárate,

Micaela Pizarro was a free colored woman of some means. In 1843, when she wrote her will, she was 40 years old and the owner of a stone house in the city with three rooms or groups of rooms (*aposentes*) for rent (probably for commercial use, such as stores); a second house, this one of wood; and seven slaves.[50] In 1844, she sold for 400 pesos the wooden house which she had built on a lot she had purchased.[51] She still owned the two houses mentioned in her 1843 will, but now she also owned three additional houses— these small, probably all made of wood, and in the new barrio of Ballajá.[52] This free colored woman appears to have been in the real estate business. She also owned a rather large number of slaves. In her will of 1843, she provided for the liberty of one of them, and a cow was to be given to two others. In a will of January 1846, she repeated the grant of liberty to one of her slaves. Two others were placed in the process of self-purchase at 300 pesos each and granted a few animals. In March 1846, Pizarro wrote another will. In this one she provided for the freedom of her remaining six slaves.[53]

In the acquisition and disposition of real property, Puerto Rico's free people of color were legally unfettered, except insofar as a long-standing racial prejudice may have undermined their ability to ac-quire wealth. Many free people of color took full advantage of their legal rights. Many acquired property through inheritance, some-times from a former master, as was the case with Fermín Sierra, "morena liberta," who acquired a small wooden house from her master.[54]

April 22, 1844, fols. 235–37. It has not been possible to determine the rate of inflation during this period. However, the figures for the 1840s reflect pesos that had been officially debased, which accounts for some part of Peña's gains.

50. Ibid., caja 501, will of Micaela Pizarro, April 24, 1843, fols. 130–130v.

51. Ibid., caja 436, record of sale, Pizarro to Vigo, June 22, 1844, fols. 193–95.

52. Ibid., caja 451, will of Micaela Pizarro, January 17, 1846, fols. 10v–11v. On the growth of the barrio of Ballajá, see Sepúlveda-Rivera, "San Juan de Puerto Rico," 411–27.

53. AGPR, PN, caja 451, will of Micaela Pizarro, September 9, 1846, fols. 186–87.

54. Ibid., caja 256, record of sale, Sierra to Tobias, February 1850, fols. 139v–41.

The full enjoyment of legal equality with regard to property ownership is illustrated also by the considerable degree to which free people of color (as well as whites) purchased and inherited parts of houses. One senses here a keen awareness of the law on the part of free people of color. In 1832, María Antonia Rodríguez, "morena libre," sold for 1,411 pesos one-half of a house that she had inherited from her father to her sister's husband.[55] In the same year, Juan Pablo de la Torre, a free colored, purchased half of a single-storied stone house for 400 pesos from the free colored woman María del Rosario Aguayo.[56] In 1835, Aguayo, born in Africa, named her daughter, Petrona Aguayo, her heir, leaving to her half of another house as well as an adult slave and the slave's three children.[57] In 1844, Ylaria Torres, free colored, sold the half of the house she had inherited from her husband, Juan Pablo de la Torre (who had purchased it in 1832 from María del Rosario Aguayo), for 500 pesos.[58] In 1853, María Lorenza Vigo, a free colored woman, purchased one-half of a single-storied stone house for 800 pesos.[59] The following year, María Gertrudis Cambián, free colored, purchased one-half of a single-storied stone house for 700 pesos.[60]

Free people of color also used the mechanism of the public auction as a means of acquiring property, as did María de la Carmen Escalera, who purchased at auction a single-storied stone house in January 1852. However, despite the fact that she was a full participant in the marketplace of property ownership, taking advantage of her legal rights, the official documents of her purchase and later

55. Ibid., caja 401, record of sale, Rodríguez to Sandoval, March 29, 1832, fols. 145–48. That Rodríguez was a *morena libre* was stated in the appended notice of satisfaction of sales tax (*alcabala*). All property figures are rounded to nearest peso.

56. Ibid., caja 481, record of sale, Aguayo to de la Torre, June 15, 1832, fols. 327–30.

57. PN, caja 485, will of María del Rosario Aguayo, July 2, 1835, fols. 398–99v.

58. PN, caja 502, record of sale, Torres to Atencio, August 14, 1844, fols. 231v–34.

59. PN, caja 260, record of sale, Poch to Vigo, January 10, 1853, fols. 14v–18.

60. PN, caja 261, record of sale, March 20, 1854, fols. 123–25.

sale of the house referred to her as a "morena libre."[61] She was still part of a caste, and not the dominant one.

The following chapters will attempt to place the absence of segregation and the considerable property ownership of the free people of color that we have seen into their proper historical context by revealing the darker side of the caste system. For the moment, and in anticipation of a later discussion of participation in the crafts, a few words are necessary about another area of considerable free colored participation in the economy.

Free people of color were involved in all San Juan trades, perhaps even dominating in some. For instance, the census for the barrio of San Juan in 1828 lists all resident carpenters, masons, and smiths. More than half of the 15 carpenters listed were free colored. At least 9 of the 11 masons were free colored. Further, it appears that there were no efforts on the part of whites to eliminate or restrict the presence of free people of color in the various trades, as indeed occurred elsewhere.[62] Not only were there free colored carpenters, masons, coopers, lathemakers, smiths, among many others, but there were also free colored silversmiths, commonly among the most prestigious of the guildsmen. Some of the free colored artisans were female. At least two were carpenters, one a shoemaker, one a barber, and one a mason. Another, the 24-year-old daughter of a silversmith, was herself a silversmith. In 1833, Juliana Carcano, originally from Africa, was a 35-year-old free colored painter.

What is one to make of all this residential freedom and economic activity among the free people of color? Clearly, we can see why many Puerto Ricans might think that their island was not a place of racism, and why the heritage of fairly benign relations between the races would lead later generations to be repelled by the racism of the

61. PN, caja 259, record of sale, Escalera to Vales, July 14, 1852, fols. 600–603.

62. See, for instance, Curry, *The Free Black in Urban America*, 18–20; Leon F. Litwack, *North of Slavery* (Chicago, 1961), 154–55, 159; Berlin, *Slaves Without Masters*, 60–61; Bowser, *The African Slave in Colonial Peru*, 142–43; and Bowser, "The Free Person of Color in Mexico City," 331–68.

United States and to desire at all costs to be disassociated from it. In this commendable absence of residential segregation and noteworthy economic achievement, however, there are clues to the true and invidious nature of the caste system. Few whites or free people of color owned their own houses in the city of San Juan, but not unexpectedly, white heads of households owned proportionately more houses, except in the one barrio of Santa Bárbara, where both races were approximately equal in ownership. When only the heads of Residential Units are considered, the relatively high degree of house ownership among free people of color in Santa Bárbara, the barrio of lowest dwelling values in 1820, suggests that ordinarily it was not initiative and desire to achieve that was lacking among free people of color, but rather economic means, at least in part a consequence of centuries of racial prejudice.

In fact, the economic performance of the free people of color was not at all as impressive as might be imagined if only opportunities of residential selection and ownership, or participation in the crafts, are considered.

4. The Demography of Caste

WE DO NOT KNOW what the free people of color thought about race relations in Puerto Rico during the early nineteenth century. It was not until the middle of the century that a few began to announce publicly their views and their prideful identity as persons of color. There were no legislative assemblies to exclude them and perhaps cause them to rise to the level of political activism; no independence movement in 1810 to grant them political benefits and models of political achievement; no political parties in Puerto Rico until after the 1868 *Grito de Lares* that might solicit their support and promise them benefits. And there were no black churches through which a political identity might have emerged. In this virtual silence, it may be concluded that free people of color as well as whites generally felt that the island suffered no serious racial problems.

To the extent that this is correct, there were several good reasons that Puerto Ricans might have thought that their society did not suffer from racial prejudice. As we saw in the case of the city of San Juan, free people of color were not segregated and had made many noteworthy achievements in the economy, especially in the crafts. Certainly, their ownership of residential buildings in the island's capital was symbolic of their active participation in the economy, of the protection offered to them by the law, and of society's liberal and tolerant attitudes.

Nevertheless, there are signs that the free people of color were disadvantaged and did not enjoy equal economic opportunity. Indications of this are the considerable degree to which ownership of

Residential Units was relegated essentially to the barrio of lowest values, Santa Bárbara, and the greater incidence of ownership by free colored women as compared to white women. This chapter peers under the veneer of economic achievement by examining the possible meaning of the way families and households were organized in San Juan.

GENDER AND AGE

The surrogate city of San Juan created from the four barrio censuses was populated by racial groups that suffered serious gender imbalance. The four censuses undercount the 0–4 and 5–9 year old cohorts, so the following discussion compensates by centering on the 15–49 age group, which appears correctly counted.[1]

The disproportion in numbers between the sexes is palpably evident when those from the ages of 15 through 49 (normal child-rearing ages) are considered, as in Table 4.1. Without in-migration,

1. The traditional way to judge gender proportions in the general population is to calculate the male-female ratio. However, the four censuses that we are dealing with severely undercounted young children, and therefore it is difficult to estimate the male-female ratio. It is now standard practice to correct for such undercounts, following Cook and Borah, and McCaa, as well as others, by applying a formula that increases the 0–4 age group by about 20 percent in relation to the 5–9 age group. See Sherburne F. Cook and Woodrow Borah, *Essays in Population History*, 2 vols. (Berkeley, Calif., 1971–1979), II, 204–13; Robert McCaa, "Women's Position, Family and Fertility Decline in Parral (Mexico) 1777–1930," *Annales de Démographie Historique* (1989), 233–43. This is a valid correction in light of standard life tables and expected age-group sizes. In the case of San Juan, however, there is the further complication that the 5–9 age cohort appears to be undercounted. The 15–49 age group emphasized here is used commonly for a variety of statistics. It is my hope that this chapter encourages others to broaden their reporting of this age group. Notwithstanding undercounts in the youth cohorts, Matos presents general population sex proportions for three barrios in 1833 and 1846 that also show a large excess of women over men (Matos, "Economy, Society and Urban Life," 98–101). For the three barrios he studied for 1833 and 1846, Matos shows roughly a 50 percent excess of women over men among free people of color (111–12; percents extrapolated from Table 2.10, 111).

Table 4.1. Number of Males Per 100 Females, Ages 15–49,
in Four San Juan Barrios, 1823–1846

	1823	1828	1833	1846
White	82.0	65.8	99.5	60.4
Free Colored	46.2	58.2	63.6	48.3

Note: Because of age-heaping and several missing ages these ratios should be considered approximations.

the free colored population of San Juan would have been in a state of demographic decline.[2] Further, the pronounced shortage of free colored males suggests that they fared poorly in the economy and had little choice but to leave the city.[3] Slave owners in Latin America

2. The matter of in-migration to urban areas is somewhat controversial. It is now clear that throughout the history of Spanish America there has been an observable and sometimes pronounced migration of peoples, including to and between urban centers (see Michael M. Swann, *Migrants in the Mexican North: Mobility, Economy, and Society in a Colonial World* [Boulder, Colo., 1989], *passim*), but it is not at all clear whether migration to urban centers tended commonly to be gender specific. John V. Lombardi has observed that in the Bishopric of Caracas, Venezuela, between 1800 and 1809 there existed a sex imbalance that may have resulted from a not unexpected migration of females to urbanized areas in search of greater economic opportunity, security, and amenities (*People and Places in Colonial Venezuela* [Bloomington, Ind., 1976], 75–82). Elizabeth Anne Kuznesof has noted a female migration to urban São Paulo (*Household Economy and Urban Development: São Paulo, 1765 to 1836* [Boulder, Colo. 1986], 83). However, as Swann has noted, it is "generally held that men were more likely to move from one town to another than were women" (Swann, *Migrants in the Mexican North*, 119). As Swann also observes, in some instances women were more likely to emigrate than men (Swann, ibid., 119–20). Further, as Andrejs Plakans and Charles Wetherell noted in the case of the peasant community of Pinkenhof, there was not only a higher degree of female in-migration but also a higher degree of female out-migration ("The Kinship Domain in an East European Peasant Community: Pinkenhof, 1833–1850," *American Historical Review* 93:2 [April 1988], 359–86). Silvia M. Arrom has noted a large female in-migration to Mexico City in 1811 and a large male out-migration. Females continued to migrate to Mexico City in considerable numbers for several decades at least (*The Women of Mexico City, 1790–1857* [Stanford, Calif., 1985], 107–11).

3. During the early nineteenth century there was an out-migration of free

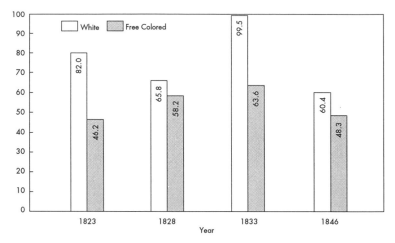

Figure 4.1. Number of Males per 100 Females, Ages 15–49, in Four San Juan Barrios, 1823–1846

were inclined to manumit females more readily than males, and to the extent that this occurred in Puerto Rico, the practice would have aggravated the gender imbalance.[4]

The barrios of San Juan were not unique in their gender imbalance. Leonard P. Curry has calculated from the general population that in fifteen urban centers in the United States during the first half of the nineteenth century, there were more free black females than males, a phenomenon which he attributes to a higher

colored people from the city of Buenos Aires to rural areas where racial restrictions appear to have been less pronounced (Marta B. Goldberg, "La población negra y mulata de la Ciudad de Buenos Aires, 1810–1840," *Desarrollo Económico* 61 [April-June 1976], 75–99, 85, note 30). Benjamín Nistal-Moret presents interesting population and age figures for whites and people of color for Manatí, Puerto Rico, for the period 1820–1851, in "El Pueblo de Nuestra Señora de la Candelaria y del Apostol San Matías de Manatí," 76–85.

4. Herbert S. Klein has observed that for Latin America and the Caribbean "all recent studies have found that approximately two-thirds of the manumitted were women (from 60 to 67%), and few were found to be 45 years of age or older" (*African Slavery in Latin America and the Caribbean* [New York, 1986], 227). According to Handler, between 1809 and 1829, 62 percent of slaves manumitted in Barbados were female (*The Unappropriated People*, 22).

mortality rate among males.[5] George Reid Andrews has noted a similar gender imbalance for Buenos Aires including all age groups. In 1810, among whites there were 103.4 males for each 100 females, and among blacks 107.9 males for each 100 females. By 1827, the differential between the sexes had worsened dramatically, when there were 90.3 white males for every 100 white females, but only 58.5 black males for every 100 black females—a sign, Andrews observes, of a "community in sharp decline and heading inexorably for extinction."[6] This was certainly due in great measure to the wars of independence, in which people of color served in large numbers. The important point here, however, is the result of this drastic gender imbalance—the demise of the community. This is not what occurred in San Juan.

Not only was there a sharp imbalance between the number of males and females among San Juan's free people of color, but there was also an imbalance in ages. The age of a population—the degree to which, for instance, it is underrepresented in its youth or in its component of child-bearing adults, or is overrepresented in its component of elderly—finely characterizes its capacity for self-generation and strongly suggests the quality of its economic performance. Many variables can affect the age of a population and its various subgroups, such as birth and death rates, and migration. It is now widely held that females have tended to live longer than males so that by the age of 25, 35, or 40, the male cohort would be

5. Curry, *The Free Black in Urban America*, 8–9. Theodore Herschberg has noted a greater number of free colored females than males in Philadelphia in 1847 ("Free-Born and Slave-Born Blacks in Antebellum Philadelphia in 1847," in Stanley L. Engerman and Eugene D. Genovese, eds., *Race and Slavery in the Western Hemisphere: Quantitative Studies* [Princeton, N.J., 1975], 410–17). Massimo Livi-Bacci has demonstrated that in Italy in 1871 and 1901 some large urban centers suffered a shortage of females rather than a shortage of males in the young age groups (*A History of Italian Fertility during the Last Two Centuries* [Princeton, N.J., 1977], 117).

6. Andrews, *The Afro-Argentines of Buenos Aires*, 74. Kuznesof presents sex ratios for the aggregate population of São Paulo for 1765, 1802, and 1836 (*Household Economy*, 82–83). See also, Nistal-Moret, "Nuestra Señora de la Candelaria," 105, for gender proportions.

smaller than its female counterpart.[7] A closeness in numbers at these ages between males and females would imply either that females were dying in abnormal numbers or were migrating out, or that males were surviving both physically and economically.[8]

Age differentials suggest a weak economic performance among San Juan's free colored males. The mean (taken here to be the measure of "average") age of the free colored population of Santa Bárbara in 1823, ages 15–49, was slightly lower than that of the white population: 28.5 years compared to 29.1 (Table 4.2). More importantly, there appears to have been a significant age difference between the sexes among free people of color. In this same age group, the mean age of free colored females in Santa Bárbara was 29.0, whereas that of free colored males was 27.5. In contrast, the mean age of white females was 29.0 and that of white males 29.2, although the mean age of both female populations was virtually the same. The youthfulness of the free colored males suggests a population in which it might have been difficult for females to find suitable mates, a point to which we shall return.

The mean ages of the free people of color and whites in the 15–49 age group in the barrio of San Juan in 1828 were almost identical, 28.7 and 28.6 respectively. As in 1823, there was now also a greater age disparity between the sexes among free people of color than among whites. The free colored women averaged 29.4 years of age, whereas the men in this population group averaged only 27.3 years. This age differential stood in sharp contrast to that of the whites, among whom males were on average 28.6 and females 28.7 years of age.

Unlike the other three barrios, in San Francisco in 1833 free people of color, ages 15–49, were on average slightly older (30.6) than whites (30.3), but again there existed an age disparity between the free colored sexes, with the males the younger group. Free col-

7. Roland Pressat, *Demographie statistique* (Paris, 1972), 22–24. See also Pressat, *Population* (tr.; London, 1970), 37, 42.

8. Because of the undercounts in the San Juan censuses, it is not possible to produce creditable age dependency ratios to determine the degree to which whites or free people of color had to support a larger percentage of "dependent" people, in this case children and the aged.

Table 4.2. Mean Age of Whites and Free People of Color Ages 15–49 in
Four San Juan Barrios, 1823–1846

	1823			1828		
	Male	Female	Total	Male	Female	Total
White	29.2	29.0	29.1	28.6	28.7	28.6
Free Colored	27.5	29.0	28.5	27.3	29.4	28.7
	1833			1846		
White	30.8	29.8	30.3	28.3	28.3	28.3
Free Colored	28.9	30.8	30.6	27.4	27.5	27.4

ored females averaged 30.8 years, whereas the males averaged 28.9.
At the same time, white females averaged 29.8 years and white
males 30.8.

In the first *trozo* of the barrio of Santo Domingo in 1846, whites
were on average older (28.3) than free people of color (27.4), but here
both racial populations manifested approximately the same mean
ages between the sexes.

The youthfulness of the free colored males as compared to free
colored females in three of the barrios suggests several fundamental questions. Was the age differential the result of economic disadvantage? Were both the age differential and economic disadvantage
the result of racial prejudice? And what effect did such age disparity
have on family and household formation? The last question shall
be considered shortly. For the moment, we shall pursue further
evidence that racial prejudice was consequential here.

RACE MIXTURE IN MARRIAGE

A fairly sensitive measure of a society's racial attitudes (and its
willingness to enforce them) is the degree to which marital partners
select mates of the same race. As would be expected in a society of
castes, whites in the city of San Juan tended overwhelmingly to
marry whites, that is, endogamously, and free people of color mar-

ried overwhelmingly among themselves. The royal decrees on marriage made it difficult for whites and free people of color under the age of consent to marry across racial lines without parental approval, thus further institutionalizing the caste system. In 1803, the Crown ruled that minors of all classes required parental permission to marry, and in 1806 the audiencia refined this intent, decreeing that "negroes, mulattos and other castes, who were minors were required to secure parental consent for marriage, just as were whites."[9] These decrees restrained marriage across caste lines, but the important point is that they did not apply to people over the age of consent or to minors when their parents did not object to the interracial marriage. The larger restraint upon such marriages was racial prejudice. In Cuba, as Verena Martinez-Alier has observed, there are many examples of colored-caste parents objecting to the marriage of their child with someone of a darker caste. She notes that "Among coloured people a very general aspiration was to become as light and to get as far away from slavery as possible."[10] This flight from slavery seems to have been universal and produced what is sometimes referred to as "color snobbery." Thus, for example, "Lightskinned freedmen formed such exclusive clubs as the Brown Fellowship Society in Charleston and proscribed social intercourse and marriage with darkskinned blacks."[11] In modern Brazil there has been a strong tendency to marry according to color line.[12]

---

9. Quoted in Martinez-Alier, *Marriage, Class and Colour,* 92.

10. Ibid., 93–98. In this regard it is beneficial to read the personal reminiscences of the Puerto Rican scholar Angela Jorge concerning the guilt a Puerto Rican woman of negroid features is made to feel for not whitening the family–*adelantar la raza.* Jorge is deeply troubled by the disdain shown by Puerto Rican men toward dark-skinned Puerto Rican women. For her, the dilemma is how to be black and Puerto Rican (as well as a woman) simultaneously. Like many other Puerto Ricans in the United States, she realizes that once she identifies with black America she becomes a black American rather than a "Puerto Rican." See Angela Jorge, "The Black Puerto Rican Woman in Contemporary American Society," in Edna Acosta-Belén, ed., *The Puerto Rican Woman: Perspectives on Culture, History, and Society* (2d ed.; New York, 1986), 180–87.

11. Toplin, *Freedom and Prejudice,* 29. It is worth noting that in Charleston, mulattoes, "Whether slave or free . . . showed contempt for the poor unedu-

The following discussion considers racial bias in mate selection in the city of San Juan. To this end, the aggregate free colored population has been differentiated to include the free colored racial categories (the subcastes) enumerated in the censuses. The discussion centers around the endogamy rate—the frequency of marriage between partners of the same race. (For a discussion of the endogamy ratio, which is more sophisticated and in some ways more interesting, see Appendix C). In all four barrios there were instances of married heads of households with no spouse enumerated, but because this is a consideration of marital pairings, these married individuals do not appear in the endogamy rates. To appreciate the full significance of these percentage rates, it is helpful to know the numbers of marriages involved, which are to be found in the tables in Appendix C.

In the barrio of Santa Bárbara, endogamy was the rule. Nearly 95 percent of white females married white males, and roughly 84 percent of the white males married white females. Yet, although these endogamy rates demonstrate overwhelming racial bias in mate selection, it is significant that 3 white females and 9 white males were married to free pardos, while 1 white male was married to a free black. In the smaller free black group, approximately 79 percent of females married free black males, whereas 95 percent of the males married endogamously. Pardos married endogamously at rates of 70.6 percent for females and 77.4 percent for males.

Perhaps not unexpectedly, racial bias in mate selection was even more strongly evident in the barrio of San Juan in 1828. White females married within their race 98.6 percent of the time, whereas white males did so 97.2 percent of the time. Yet, 1 white woman and 2 white males married free pardos.[13] Free pardos and free blacks

---

cated whites" (ibid.). I have seen no indication that such attitudes existed in Puerto Rico, but I would be surprised if they did not. For a discussion of the attitudes of lightskinned people of color toward those darker skinned, see Andrews, *Blacks and Whites in São Paulo*, 177–80.

12. Degler, *Neither Black nor White*, 186–87. For an informative discussion of this issue in Jamaica, see Fernando Henriques, *Family and Colour in Jamaica* (2d ed.; London, 1968), 49, 52–53, 57–58.

13. For the barrio of San Juan in 1828, the census enumerators used the

also generally married within their own racial subcastes. No free black female was married to a white male, but 2 pardo females were married to whites.

Racial bias in the selection of marital partners was extremely strong in the barrio of San Francisco in 1833, and within several groups absolute. White females chose white males as mates in more than 98 percent of their marriages, and white males chose white females as mates in every one of theirs.[14] One hundred percent of the mulatto women married mulatto men, and 89.5 percent of the mulatto men married mulatto women. The largest free colored group in the barrio of San Francisco, the blacks, also displayed a strong racial bias in mate selection, with nearly 94 percent of the females and 97 percent of the males marrying within this subcaste. Similarly, the pardos manifested decided racial bias in their pairings, with 100 percent of the females selecting pardo males and 83.3 percent of the pardo males choosing pardo females.

Thus, an almost absolute racial bias was at work in the selection of marriage partners not only among the whites, but also within the various free colored subcastes. Among the four barrios studied, the barrio of San Francisco displayed the greatest sense of racial stratification and consciousness. It is certain that the free colored population here was equally or just about as racially biased as the whites. That the free people of color did not, save with rare exception, marry whites was clearly not entirely of their own doing, but that they largely chose to marry according to a racial categorization based on degree of whiteness (or blackness)—a categorization set upon them by the white establishment—was indeed of their own doing, and was a tribute to the efficacy of the caste system.[15]

---

letters M for pardo and N for moreno, as is made clear in the census summation, f. 146.

14. The nomenclature used in the barrio of San Francisco was rather unusual. The pardo group was the smallest among the free people of color, when ordinarily one would expect it to be the largest. Furthermore, the pardos, as generally the free people of lightest skin color, would presumably have been labelled *mulatto* in the 1833 typology. It is probable that the San Francisco enumerators used the term *mulatto* as others would have used *pardo*.

15. There is certainly confirmation here of H. Hoetink's much quoted obser-

The racial bias of whites and free people of color alike in choosing marriage partners is further confirmed by the pairings in the
barrio of Santo Domingo (first *trozo*) in 1846. All white females
selected white males for their mates, and almost 95 percent of the
white males chose white females. Only 6 *grifos* were married in the
first *trozo*, and they formed 3 endogamous pairs. (*Grifo* was a term
widely used by the middle of the nineteenth century to categorize
those we might refer to as "high yellow"—that is, a person of Negroid phenotype with nearly white complexion and hair some-
where between kinky and straight.[16]) There were 2 moreno endogamous marriages, but 1 black woman was married to a moreno
man.[17] Ninety percent of the married black females chose black
males, and all of the married black males married black females.
Likewise, all of the married pardo males married pardo females, but
only three-fourths of the married pardo females chose pardo males,
two having married white males. Thus, although there was indeed

---

vation that "the lower-placed segment cannot, for psychological reasons, fail to
view the dominant segment's physical characteristics as actually superior or to
adopt this segment's standards regarding what is beautiful and ugly (*The Two
Variants in Caribbean Race Relations* [tr.; New York, 1967], 134–35). There is
also general confirmation of Rust and Seed's observation that "Large groups
with balanced sex ratios are considerably more endogamous and less apt to
intermarry than smaller groups with imbalanced sex ratios. More importantly,
even in a relatively large group the sex with the fewer potential partners may be
forced to seek partners outside the groups" (Rust and Seed, "Equality of Endogamy," 74). However, as we see, small groups could be highly endogamous.

16. Personal communication from Luis de la Rosa, May 30, 1986. André
Pierre Ledrú recorded that a *grifo* was the product of a union between a "Mulatto" and a "Negra" (*Viaje a la Isla de Puerto Rico*, 112), but this definition is
highly unlikely by the 1840s. For the twentieth-century use of the term, see
Roger, "The Role of Semantics," 451. The quality of hair did not play as salient a
role in Puerto Rican racial prejudice as it did in some other Caribbean islands
such as Jamaica. For the place of color and hair quality in Jamaican racial prejudice, see Fernando Henriques, *Family and Colour in Jamaica*, 54–57. Based
especially on his knowledge of Jamaica, Orlando Patterson renders the highly
debatable generalization that "it was not so much color differences as differences in hair type that become critical as a mark of servility in the Americas"
(*Slavery and Social Death*, 61).

17. In this instance, I am presuming that by the letter M the census enumerators meant moreno rather than mulatto.

some racial mixing in the barrio of Santo Domingo, the preponderant tendency was to marry within one's race, that is, to display strong racial bias in selecting a mate.

When whites and free people of color in the city of San Juan are considered as two racial groups, it is evident that on the whole both groups married among themselves (Figure 4.2).[18] This propensity to endogamy was abetted by the gender imbalance we have observed. White males did not outnumber white females; consequently, they had no demographic impulsion toward rampant racial intermixture. Likewise, the shortage of free colored males meant that few were demographically impelled to seek white marital mates.[19] However, a considerable number of whites, both males and females, married free people of color, attesting to a racial prejudice that was both surmountable and complex in its conception and application.

The matter of bias in mate selection is central to an understand-

18. During the period 1646–1746 in the parish of Santa Veracruz in Mexico City, "Negroes . . . exhibited a marked tendency to marry either Negroes or mulattoes . . . [whereas] marriage patterns of the male and female mulattoes was (sic) more diversified than that of their Negro counterparts (Edgar F. Love, "Marriage Patterns of Persons of African Descent in a Colonial Mexico City Parish," *HAHR* 51:1 [Feb. 1971], 79–91). For marital patterns in late colonial Veracruz, Mexico, see Carroll, *Blacks in Colonial Veracruz*, 120–24.

19. Winthrop Jordan has argued that a central reason Barbados was more racially restrictive than Jamaica during the era of slavery was that there were fewer white males than white females in Barbados, whereas there were many more white males than white females in Jamaica. In this circumstance, it seems logical that white males in Jamaica would and in fact did cohabit with women of color more readily than occurred in Barbados, where in theory white males could find suitable white females. See Jordan, "American Chiaroscuro," *William and Mary Quarterly* 19 (April 1962), 183–200; and *White over Black: American Attitudes toward the Negro, 1550–1812* (pb.; Baltimore, Md., 1969), 175–78. David Brion Davis generally subscribes to Jordan's argument, concluding that "it seems probable that sex ratio and the proportion of slaves were at least as important as nationality in shaping attitudes toward the manumission and treatment of mulattoes" (*The Problem of Slavery*, 273, n. 20). In San Juan, the white male deficit was offset by the free colored male deficit, meaning that although the whites maintained a policy of racial restriction, it did not have to be harsh. Even when free colored men married white females, there were enough of the latter to satisfy the marital needs of the white males.

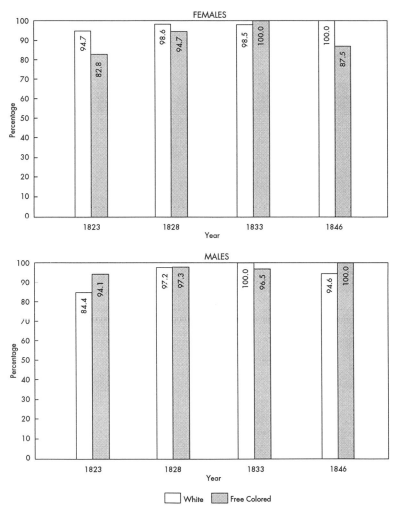

Figure 4.2. Endogamy Rates in Four San Juan Barrios, 1823–1846

ing of the nature and evolution of Puerto Rican racial prejudice and deserves further comment. Church registers for the Parish of Nuestra Señora de los Remedios, which encompassed the barrios of San Juan and Santa Bárbara and was centered in the Cathedral of San Juan, corroborate marital patterns evident in the census of 1828.

In 1828, 13 marriages were performed in the Cathedral of San

Juan in which at least one partner was a free person of color. In 4 of those marriages, *morenos libres* married *morenos libres*. In 8 other marriages *pardos libres* married *pardos libres*. In the remaining marriage a free moreno man married a slave.[20] Obviously, racial preference was a strong factor in mate selection in the Parish of Los Remedios in 1828. However, marriages in 1829 were less endogamous. In that year, *pardos libres* were involved in 17 marriages, 13 occurring within their subcaste. One *parda libre* married a white man; 1 married a slave; another married a *moreno libre*; and 1 *pardo libre* married a *morena libre*. There was even less endogamy among the *morenos libres*. Eight *moreno libre* males married, but 2 did not marry within the subcaste. One *morena libre* married a *pardo libre*.[21]

The marriage records for the Parish of Los Remedios in 1828 and 1829 confirm two very important facts of Puerto Rican life. The figures for 1828 confirm the racially inspired patterns of marital preference recorded longitudinally in the civil census of that year. The figures for 1829 confirm the absence of legal coercion to marry within the subcastes.

Racial bias in mate selection had its origins in Spanish racism as mediated by the Puerto Rican colonial experience. Clearly, the people of color had adopted the logic of the caste system, which argues compellingly that there were decided social (and perhaps economic) advantages to protecting against darkening the family's skin color. This racial bias in mate selection may have had a direct effect on the nature of free colored families and households. The difference between the mean ages of free colored males and females in three of the four barrios studied may have made it difficult for some females to find suitable marital or consensual partners. Moreover, the age differentials within the subcastes were sometimes of even greater magnitude. The largest subcaste in the barrio of Santa Bárbara in 1823 was the *pardos libres*. The mean age of males and females in the 15–49 age group was virtually the same. Among the

20. AHD, Archivo Catedral, libro 6, Matrimonios Pardos, 1818–1836.
21. Ibid. In four additional marriages no race was given, and in a fifth the description was unclear.

next largest subcaste, the *negros libres,* however, males were on average 3.6 years younger than females. Given the logic of racial prejudice in the city of San Juan, some *negro libre* females may have found it difficult to find suitable (in the sense of age and therefore perhaps economic achievement) marital or consensual mates. Similarly, in the barrio of San Juan in 1828, the males of one subcaste were on average 3.7 years younger than the females.[22]

Racial prejudice harmed San Juan's free people of color in diverse

22. It is not until 1846 and the first *trozo* of the barrio of Santo Domingo that we encounter males on average older than the females in their subcaste. For a discussion of age imbalances in marriage, see E. A. Wrigley, *Population and History* (New York, 1969), 102–6. Although one must be very cautious in generalizing about the significance of marital age differences, it appears normal in the West that in wealthy families males were older than their brides at marriage, with the gap narrowing among poorer families. The San Juan pattern suggests free colored male impoverishment. Matos has estimated the age at first marriage for those in the three barrios he studied for 1833 and 1846, and he concluded that in 1833 free women married "on average, almost four years younger than men" and in 1846 "almost three (3) years earlier than free men" ("Economy, Society and Urban Life," 150–51). He also observes that "San Juan's residents were very close to the typical ages of marriage in rural Western European areas: 25–26 years for women and 27–28 for men" (151). (To produce his data, Matos employed the inferential Singulate Mean Age at Marriage statistic [see Colin Newell, *Methods and Models in Demography* (London, 1988, 97–101)]). I did not use this statistic because the 0–15 cohort is essential to its logic, and as the reader knows there is a problem with the undercounts in this cohort in the censuses I studied. There were also undercounts in the censuses Matos studied. He writes: "Finally, there was a significant lack of children ages 1 through 10 among all groups, even when accounting for under-reporting" (113). Indeed. For the European ages, Matos has relied on the seminal essay by J. Hajnal, "European Marriage Patterns in Perspective," in D. V. Glass and D. E. C. Eversley, *Population in History* (London, 1965), 101–43; and on Michael Anderson, *Approaches to the History of the Western Family, 1500–1914* (London, 1980). Hajnal's essay is highly recommended, not least because it offers data also on nonrural areas and the Mediterranean region. Assuming the validity of Matos's statistical method, his figures further demonstrate how difficult it would have been for free women of color to find suitable mates. Matos has also suggested that one reason for fewer marriages among free colored women was the high costs of sacramental fees for marriage (156). It is reasonable to assume that these fees did militate against formal marriage by the very poor (regardless of race), and if so there is further proof that impoverishment played a very broad role in family formation.

ways. Sometimes the harm was overt and clear, as when they were deprived of educational and bureaucratic opportunities. Sometimes it was more subtle, as when they adopted the racial logic of the white establishment and married within their subcastes. Sometimes it may not have been apparent at all, as when their own racial prejudices contributed to making it difficult for some women to find suitable mates.

This discussion has emphasized the degree to which the San Juan castes married within themselves, but it has also noted some exceptions. The exceptions are important because they remind us that racial prejudice in Puerto Rico in many ways was not extreme and had evolved in its own particular manner. To add a dimension of humanity to the marital statistics—to put faces on the numbers—it is worthwhile to explore some examples of intermarriage. In the barrio of San Juan in 1828, Gregorio Rosado, 41 and white, was living with María Josefa Abendano, 38 and free colored. Both were single. (Interestingly, Rosado was enumerated without the honorific.) Another racially mixed unwed couple were a 38-year-old white cordage-maker and his 32-year-old free colored concubine. Also residing in the barrio of San Juan in 1828 were Don Lorenzo Kelht, a 51-year-old white watchmaker from Austria, and his 36-year-old free colored concubine, Juana Trillo. They had three children, apparently theirs together, and all free colored. In Spanish America, following the principle of hypo descent, children of racially mixed parents normally inherited the race of the parent legally considered racially "inferior." According to Martinez-Alier, this was always the case in Cuba.[23] However, the rule of hypo descent was loosely applied in the city of San Juan (except when the mother was a slave).

The matter of hypo descent is of particular interest because it communicates a society's attitude toward race mixing. Although there are many examples of children inheriting the racial classification of their racially "inferior" parent, as one would expect, there

23. Martinez-Alier, *Marriage, Class and Colour,* 17. For a comparative discussion of racial inheritance, see Patterson, *Slavery and Social Death,* 132–47.

are also examples to the contrary. For instance, in 1833 in the barrio of San Francisco, a 41-year-old single free colored woman had a 19-year-old single white son. In 1846, in the barrio of Santo Domingo, Juan José Landa, 24 and white, was married to Juana Ramona Negrón, 32 and free colored. They had a 12-year-old son, enumerated as white. Clearly, the boy was not Landa's child, but in any event did not inherit the racial classification of his racially "inferior" parent. Also living in Santo Domingo was Don Rupeto Hernández, a 28-year-old white sacristan who was married to a 20-year-old free "black" woman. They had two young children, both white.

Two instances of race mixing within families are unusual and illuminating. In 1846, Julian Carmona was a 40-year-old free colored carpenter living in the barrio of Santo Domingo with his 39-year-old free colored wife. They had 5 free colored children, ranging in age from 15 to 4, but also living with them was Manuela Ruiz, a 24-year-old white female enumerated along with the Carmona children. Biologically, she could have been the child of Carmona's wife from a previous relationship, or she could have been an adopted child. If the former, then the child did not inherit the racial classification of her mother. If the latter, then we see the willingness of a racially "inferior" couple to raise a racially "superior" child, presumably without governmental interference. Also in the barrio of Santo Domingo in 1846 resided Doña Rosa Berouete, a 55-year-old free colored widow from the island of Santo Domingo, and her 13-year-old adopted white daughter, likewise from Santo Domingo. Doña Rosa was not only the head of a racially mixed family, but also the head of a Residential Unit which comprised a free colored renter and a white renter. That she was raising a white child must have been socially acceptable.

For their part, whites sometimes just as openly raised children of a different race, in this instance, of course, an "inferior" race. In the barrio of San Juan in 1828, for example, a 30-year-old white man was married to a 25-year-old white woman. They had a free colored child, but one with a different family name, suggesting that she was the wife's daughter from a previous relationship or the couple's adopted daughter. The family rented rooms in a house owned by a white widow, who also resided in the dwelling. In 1833, in the barrio of San Francisco, a 55-year-old free colored man, and his 35-year-old white wife had two children, 20 and 17, both free colored. Perhaps one or both were not hers. This white woman, nevertheless, was married to a free colored man and was raising free colored children. It is interesting that the father was a free "black" and the children were free mulattoes, a racial classification closer to white. In 1846, in the barrio of Santo Domingo, a 26-year-old married white woman lived with her two young free colored children.[24]

These exceptions to the degrading rigidities of Puerto Rican racial prejudice were only that, but they nevertheless existed and need to be counted as part of the island's racial mentality.

BIRTH AND DEATH

Birth and death rates are often revealing indexes of a particular population's economic condition, or one might say, performance.[25]

24. Puerto Ricans in the island and in the United States tend to take pride in their willingness to adopt children without regard to race, and not always with legal sanction. In the latter case, the children are known as *hijos de crianza*, and their presence in Puerto Rican society obviously goes back deep into the nineteenth century and perhaps beyond (see Rodríguez, *Puerto Ricans*, 55).

25. The standard formula for determining birth and death rates is the number of births or deaths during a year divided by the population and then multiplied by 1,000. The result is the Crude Birth or Death Rate. The rates are especially useful for comparative purposes.

Because the young were undercounted in the four San Juan censuses studied, it is not possible to infer fertility rates by comparing children ages 0–4 to females ages 15–49, as is commonly done. Puerto Rico did not provide for the civil registry of births, deaths, and marriages until 1885, which leaves Church registers a possible source of information. However, the Church registers for the Parish of Los Remedios (barrios of San Juan and Santa Bárbara) are not useful in calculating the traditionally used Crude Birth Rate because there are coterminous population figures for only San Juan in 1828 and not Santa Bárbara. In that year, 116 white and 98 free colored infants were baptized in the Cathedral. Even if we estimated a population for Santa Bárbara in 1828 and employed baptisms as surrogates for births, as is often done, the Crude Birth Rate for whites and free people of color would be so unrealistically high that it would have to be concluded that parents from outside the parish brought children to

It is possible to estimate birth and death rates for Puerto Rico for the early nineteenth century from the account of Colonel George Flinter, an Irish officer in the Spanish military, who, according to his own statement, copied vital statistics exactly from the monthly official returns made to the colony's Captain General. Calculating from Flinter's figures for the year 1828 produces a Crude Birth Rate of 35.8 for whites and 55.1 for the free people of color.[26] These figures are roughly what one would expect for a largely rural, agricultural society.[27]

the Cathedral for baptism, which certainly would have been unremarkable. (However, this should serve as a caution to those scholars who consider baptisms the equivalent of births, especially when studying only a single year.)

Death rates cannot be calculated for the barrios of San Juan and Santa Bárbara for an additional reason. All deaths were recorded in the same book—whites, free people of color, and slaves. It is common to consider all decedents not labeled as people of color to have been white. This approach cannot work for San Juan, where many deceased people of color were not labeled as such. Employing the standard method would produce the lowest death rate perhaps ever recorded. See, for example, AHD, Archivo Catedral, Difunciones, 1826–1831. (For problems with racial identification in Church registers, see Luisa Géigel De Gandía, La genealogía y el apellido de Campeche [San Juan, 1972], 6–9, 41). One should be especially suspicious of all the *hijos naturales* not depicted as people of color in the Libros de Difunciones. I have also examined the registers of births, deaths, and marriages, of the Parroquia Nuestra Señora de Guadalupe, Catedral, for Ponce for the year 1860 (microfilm, Family History Library, the Church of Jesus Christ of Latter-Day Saints, reels 820695, 820702, 820704, 820708), that I hoped to use with a civil census of Ponce for that year. However, racial classifications were not recorded in the Church records.

26. Flinter, *An Account of the Present State of the Island of Puerto Rico*, 214–17.

27. Vásquez Calzada estimates a birth rate considerably higher for the period on the basis of estimated errors of omission. See *La población de Puerto Rico*, 114, 116. In the era before modern birth control, Crude Birth Rates normally averaged between 35 and 55 per 1,000 and Crude Death Rates between 30 and 40 per 1,000. See Stuart B. Schwartz, *Sugar Plantations in the Formation of Brazilian Society: Bahia, 1550–1835* (pb.; Cambridge, Eng., 1989), 367. In Minas Gerais, Brazil, the Crude Birth Rate in 1814 for the free colored was 42 per 1,000 and for whites 37 per 1,000. The death rates in that year were 34 per 1,000 for the free colored and 27 per 1,000 for whites (Klein, *African Slavery*, 230). For a comparison with eleven Latin American countries between 1930 and 1960, see Eduardo E. Arriaga, *Mortality Decline and Its Demographic Effects in Latin America* (Berkeley, Calif., 1970), 147–48.

Unfortunately, there exists very little information on births and deaths in the civil documents for San Juan. However, there is some useful, albeit fragmentary, information. During the first six months of 1843, for instance, the capital's white population had a birth to death ratio of 1.14, while the free colored population witnessed more deaths than births, for a ratio of 0.78.[28]

More complete data are available for San Juan for the year 1858. Then, the birth to death ratio for free people of color was a healthier 1.30. However, the capital's white population was doing far more than just sustaining itself, with a birth to death ratio of 2.38.[29]

The birth and death rates for San Juan conform to what apparently was a universal phenomenon: people of color tended to have higher birth and death rates than did whites.[30] The degree to which

28. AGPR, Gobernadores, Municipales, San Juan, 1840–1845, caja 568, entry 300, pliego trimestre, 1843. Without a population figure for San Juan in or around 1843, Crude Birth and Death Rates cannot be calculated.

29. The civil account of births and deaths for San Juan for 1858 was signed on the last day of the following year, suggesting an error in either the date 1858 or 1859. This is of some consequence because there are no population figures for San Juan for either 1858 or 1859, but there are figures for 1860, when an island-wide census was conducted and soon published (Censo de la población de 1860, La Gaceta, August 20, 1861). Employing the 1860 population figures, it is possible to calculate Crude Birth and Death Rates per 1,000 inhabitants for the city of San Juan for 1858 (or 1859), but these must be considered approximations. In this circumstance, the Crude Birth Rate for whites was 21.0 and for free people of color 37.1. The Crude Death Rate for whites was 8.8 and for free people of color 28.0. These birth and death rates are roughly within the range estimated by Vásquez Calzada for Puerto Rico for the period 1888–1898 (La población de Puerto Rico, 116–17), with the exception of the Crude Death Rate for whites for 1858. Clearly, the death rate for whites was remarkably low, and it must be considered the result of an undercount. Birth and death rates can be found also in Mario A. Rodríguez León, Los registros parroquiales y la microhistoria demográfica en Puerto Rico (San Juan, 1990), passim.

30. This has been the case in the United States. For fertility rates in recent United States history, see Andrew Hacker, Two Nations: Black and White, Separate, Hostile, Unequal (pb.; New York, 1993), 71; and Andrew Billingsley, Climbing Jacob's Ladder: The Enduring Legacy of African-American Families (New York, 1992), 148. Fernando Picó provides birth figures for Río Piedras and Utuado, 1765–1807, in Historia general de Puerto Rico (5th ed.; Río Piedras, P.R., 1990), 136, and death figures for whites and free people of color following a cholera epidemic in Río Piedras (now a part of the city of San Juan, and the

Table 4.3. Crude Birth and Death Rates for Seven Puerto Rican Towns
in 1858

	Birth Rate*		Death Rate*	
TOWN	Whites	Free Colored	Whites	Free Colored
Patillas	22.5	67.0	11.2	38.2
Salinas	35.6	79.6	32.5	56.3
Río Grande	25.3	63.5	18.7	32.2
Aguadilla	40.5	82.9	22.0	38.4
Arecibo	49.1	90.4	16.7	71.7
Aguda	23.0	42.1	25.5	58.0
Trugillo Alto	30.0	101.4	27.0	48.3

*Rate per 1000.
Note: These figures collapse free "mulattoes" with a much smaller free "Negro"
population. I have corrected for out-migrants because they could not have died in the
particular town.
Source: AGPR, Gobernadores, Censo y Riqueza, caja 16.

this disparity reflects economic status remains unclear for San
Juan. What is especially important is the degree to which each race
was able to sustain its numbers. At times, free colored death rates
in Puerto Rico were alarmingly high; yet they were not demographically catastrophic. It has been possible to compile systematic
data on births and deaths for seven Puerto Rican towns in 1858
(Table 4.3). In each instance, the free colored population had much
higher death rates than did the whites. Yet, because of high birth
rates, the free colored were capable of replenishing their numbers.
In fact, for the seven towns the aggregate birth to death ratios for
whites and free people of color was, remarkably in the face of the
high death rates, almost exactly the same: 1.65 for the whites and
1.63 for the free people of color. Even Arecibo, with the highest free
colored death rate among the seven towns, managed a favorable
birth to death ratio of 1.26.[31]

location of the University of Puerto Rico) for 1856 and 1857, in *Vivir en Caimito*
(2d ed.; Río Piedras, P.R., 1989), 33.

31. AGPR, Gobernadores, Censo y Riqueza, caja 16.

The data on birth and death rates compel two questions. Were the high birth and death rates among the free people of color attributable to conditions engendered by racial prejudice? And did the pattern of high births and deaths affect the ability of free people of color to form and sustain families and households? It is widely held that there is a direct and causal relationship between low economic status and high birth and death rates. Because most free people of color in Puerto Rico were in the lowest economic stratum, there seems to be a good fit here also between economics and birth and death rates.[32] It is a central argument of this book that such phenomena were to a considerable extent the result of racial prejudice—in this case, as it limited the possibilities for economic betterment. As to the second question, the free people of color of Puerto Rico did in fact manage to form and sustain families and households, although in San Juan, as shall be seen in the following chapter, most of them were headed by single females.

32. As Klein observes, it is because "of pervasive poverty that the free colored in all American slave societies typically had the highest mortality and disease rates among the free populations" (*African Slavery*, 230).

5. Household and Family
in San Juan

THE SIZE AND CONFIGURATION of households and families have been of paramount importance to scholars, politicians, and social reformers during the past several decades, and are central to an understanding of racial prejudice and discrimination. Most of the data and the conclusions drawn from them are at best suggestive, at worst inflammatory. Nevertheless, certain things can be agreed upon, such as the simple fact that at the lower levels of the economy a family with two wage earners is likely to be better off economically than a family with one wage earner. This uncontroversial statement has been made by scholars dealing with recent United States social and racial history. Although it is always dangerous for scholars to consider their data within the context of another culture, especially one distant in time and dissimilar in economic development, the data for Puerto Rico can be placed within the context of the social and racial experience of the United States. Certain facts, such as the above statement about wage earners, can cross time and boundaries without straining the benefits of cross-cultural analysis.

Despite a lack of standardized terminology, the initial studies of the Latin American household during the eighteenth and nineteenth centuries suggest an average size of between four and six free people, with both the socioeconomic and racial status of the head of the household or family affecting its size.[1] For instance, José Luis

1. Linda L. Greenow summarizes the literature and data in "Spatial Dimensions of Household and Family in Eighteenth-Century Spanish America," 12–15. See also Elizabeth Kuznesof and Robert Oppenheimer, "The Family and

Moreno has shown that in Buenos Aires in 1778, the more affluent occupational groups had larger households, slaves included, than did the less affluent.[2] Linda L. Greenow has concluded that in areas of Cartagena (New Granada), which she studied for 1777, whites had larger households than did "coloreds or Negroes."[3] Elizabeth Anne Kuznesof has shown a somewhat smaller mean household size for the urban area of São Paulo in 1802 (4.20) and 1836 (3.76).[4] In both years, elite households were substantially larger.[5] The data for

Society in Nineteenth-Century Latin America: An Historiographical Introduction," *Journal of Family History* 10:3 (fall 1985), 215–35. For a standard example of European interest in the family, see Peter Laslett, ed., *Household and Family in Past Time* (pb.; Cambridge, Eng., 1974), 1–89. Examples of the questions asked about the Latin American family, and some answers, are in David J. Robinson, "The Analysis of Eighteenth-Century Spanish American Cities: Some Problems and Alternative Solutions" (discussion paper no. 4, Department of Geography, Syracuse University, 1975), *passim.*; Greenow, "Spatial Dimensions of Household and Family Structure," 3–15; Donald Ramos, "Marriage and the Family in Colonial Vila Rica," *HAHR* 55:2 (May 1975), 200–225; Ramos, "Vila Rica: Profile of a Colonial Brazilian Center," *The Americas* 35:4 (April 1979), 495–526; Michael M. Swann, *Tierra Adentro*, 247–60; José Luis Moreno, "La estructura social y demográfica de la Ciudad de Buenos Aires en el año 1778," *Anuario del Instituto de Investigaciones Históricas*, 8 (1965), 151–70.

2. Moreno, "La Estructura Social," 151–70; Robinson, "Analysis of Eighteenth-Century Cities," 29–33. See also, Mark D. Szuchman, "Household Structure and Political Crisis: Buenos Aires, 1810–1860," *LARR* 21:3 (1986), 55–93. It is of great interest that Massimo Livi-Bacci has shown that in premodern Italy the affluent had larger families than did the poor and that this pattern reversed itself in the modern era (*A History of Italian Fertility*, 218–27).

3. Greenow, "Family, Household and Home," 43. However, Robinson has calculated that in Río Negro (New Granada) in 1787, negroes, mulattoes, and mestizos appear to have had a greater percentage of large households than did whites (mentioned in Ibid., 17–18).

4. Kuznesof, *Household Economy*, 156. For Latin America as a whole, Kuznesof notes that "The most obvious consistent finding among household studies is that the average household in the eighteenth and nineteenth centuries was relatively small (between four and six free members), both in urban and rural areas" (Elizabeth Kuznesof, "Household and Family Studies," in K. Lynn Stoner, ed., *Latinas of the Americas: A Source Book* [New York, 1989], 305–37, 308).

5. Ibid., 165. Kuznesof's definition of *elite* eliminates many households that

Table 5.1. Mean Household Size by Race in Four San Juan Barrios,
1823–1846 (Uncorrected)

	1823	1828	1833	1846
White	4.6	4.7	4.9	4.5
Free Colored	3.5	2.7	2.5	2.6

mean household size for the city of San Juan fall within the order of magnitude seen elsewhere.

For this discussion it is worthwhile to use the full undercounted San Juan censuses. In these censuses the mean household size among whites in the four San Juan barrios was marginally less than the typical five to six person households counted elsewhere (Table 5.1). (As mentioned, *household* here means coresident family of one or more persons plus relatives, guests, employees, and slaves.) A valid count of the 0–9 cohort would bring these household figures fairly much in line with what appears to have been a normal household size in the rest of Latin America. However, it seems safe to presume that, even with a valid count, the mean household size among San Juan's free people of color would be markedly less than among whites.[6] In San Juan, this was almost certainly a consequence of less affluence. Further, in each instance the size of the white nuclear family was on average larger than that of the free colored (Table 5.2), but not by very much. A valid count in the 0–9 cohort would probably have kept them very close in size. The nuclear family is the conjugal or consensual family unit, with solitaries (and widows with children) not included. Since the nuclear families were fairly close in size, the question arises as to why the white households were noticeably larger than those of the

---

might have owned few or no slaves; therefore, a more expansive categorization of *elite* would have produced somewhat smaller elite households.

6. The data in Tables 5.1 and 5.2 were rendered through standard coding technique. That is, the first named person in each household was taken to be the head of household. For additional family-size figures for the barrios he studied, see Matos, "Economy, Society and Urban Life," 139–41.

Table 5.2. Mean Nuclear Family Size by Race in Four San Juan Barrios,
1823–1846 (Uncorrected)

	1823	1828	1833	1846
White	3.7	4.3	3.5	3.8
Free Colored	3.6	3.1	2.9	3.5

Note: There were very few agregado families and they are not included in these figures.

free people of color. Greater affluence among whites may have permitted them to keep older children at home longer than the free people of color were able to do.[7] In any event, whites owned more slaves.

Household size in the city of San Juan was affected by the ability or desire to own slaves. Unfortunately, it is not always possible to determine precisely who in the household owned the slaves enumerated. Slaves sometimes appeared at the bottom of a household list and it must be presumed that in some instances it was not the head of the household but rather one of the agregados who owned the slaves.[8] Clearly, however, white households were larger in part due to a higher degree of slave ownership, which can be taken as a sign of greater economic well-being.[9]

7. Greenow makes this point for Cartagena in 1777 ("Family, Household and Home," 15).

8. As mentioned, agregados could be boarders, guests, or domestics.

9. Whites also supported more agregados than did free people of color, although only fractionally. In fact, there were relatively few agregados in the four barrios, averaging less than one per white or free colored household. Nonetheless, when the agregados are combined with the more than one slave per white household, the difference in the mean household sizes becomes explicable.

Following Kuznesof, Matos observes that the "large presence of agregados in Latin American cities has been connected to high levels of poor and female-headed households," and he believes this to have been the case for San Juan also (Matos, "Economy, Society and Urban Life," 144; Kuznesof, "Household and Family Studies," 305–37, 312–13). No doubt the taking in of friends and relatives was a way for the poor to share the burdens of life, and this social sharing did indeed take place in San Juan. However, many affluent families took in friends, relatives, and boarders who themselves were often people of affluence. This applies to free people of color as well as to whites.

The number of children among white and free colored families is an extremely important clue to economic achievement. The average family in the barrios studied had approximately one and a half resident children. In a valid count of the 0–9 cohort, this figure obviously would have been greater. What is especially interesting is that among whites more male-headed families tended to have from 1 to 4 children than occurred among free people of color, among whom more female-headed families had children in this range. Furthermore, in almost every case these female-headed families were single-parent families.[10]

To the extent that there is a pattern, the question is, why among whites did more male-headed families tend to have more children than did female-headed families, whereas the reverse was true among free colored families? Two answers seem plausible. First, greater economic opportunity for white males made it possible for more of them to have maintained families and produce children than was the case among free colored males. Hence, the racially defined economic reality made it quite natural for more white males than white females to have headed child-producing families. This was unquestionably a salutary circumstance. On the other hand, among free people of color, it was more difficult for males to head and maintain child-producing families than their white male counterparts. Thus, heading child-producing families, both marital and consensual, devolved upon the free colored females (Table 5.3). Second, as we have seen, there existed an unwholesome age differential between the sexes within some of the free colored subcastes, with males being younger on average than females, an imbalance that would have left more females than males to head families with the model number of children.

10. To put it another way, with 4 years studied and 4 values for each year (1, 2, 3, or 4 children), there are 16 possible observations for each race. From this perspective, white male-headed families had 1–4 children 9 times to the females' 6 times, the sexes having had the same number of children once. However, female-headed families among free people of color had 1–4 children 14 out of a possible 16 times, they also having had the same number of children as their male counterparts once. Altogether, the elements of a pattern seem to be in place here.

Table 5.3. Percent of All Female-Headed Families with Children Present
in Four San Juan Barrios, 1823–1846 (Uncorrected)

	1823	1828	1833	1846
White	42.3	52.5	38.7	47.0
Free Colored	65.3	64.6	66.7	67.2

Is this phenomenon—more white male-headed families having from 1 to 4 children than occurred among free people of color, in whose case female-headed families had this number of children—an echo of the undercounts in the four censuses? Almost certainly not. A normal distribution of children among whites and free people of color, male and female, would have had little or no effect on this pattern.

The barrio of San Juan was an exception. San Juan was the barrio most prestigious for business and costly in real estate. It is plausible that a considerable number of white males were unable to survive the economic challenge of this barrio. Thus, it may also have been economics that caused more white female-headed families than male-headed families in the barrio of San Juan to have had 1 to 4 children.[11]

The degree to which females headed households in the city of San Juan is simply startling. But this applies to whites as well as to free people of color. In the barrio of Santa Bárbara in 1823, 62.6 percent of free colored households were headed by single females, while among whites 33.3 percent were similarly headed. In the barrio of San Juan in 1828, 57.7 percent of free colored households were headed by single females. In the barrio of San Francisco in 1833, the percent of single female–headed households among free people of color reached a remarkable 66.5 percent, whereas 36.6 percent of white households were single female–headed. In the first *trozo* of the barrio of Santo Domingo in 1846, 64 percent of free col-

---

11. It should be noted that the undercount in the 0–9 cohort was especially sharp in the barrio of San Francisco in 1833.

ored households were single female–headed, while among whites the incidence reached an extremely high 50.7 percent.[12] It is worthwhile to consider these proportions in the context of another slave city, the urban area of São Paulo, Brazil, in 1802 and 1836. The incidence of single female–headed households among whites and blacks combined was 44.7 percent in 1802, and in 1836, 39.3 percent. As Kuznesof has observed, "these are extremely high rates of female headship for a western society at any known time."[13]

What was the cause of the extraordinary degree of single female family and household headship among the free people of color in the city of San Juan? It may well be that single female-headship resulted in part from affluence among some whites and free colored,[14] perhaps especially so among free colored females, who, because of gender and age imbalances, may have found it difficult to find suitable mates. Nevertheless, until we have contrary proof, it is prudent to presume that the degree to which so many single free colored females headed families and households was the social embodiment of widespread marginal economic performance.[15]

12. For generally confirming data from the barrios he studied, see Matos, "Economy, Society and Urban Life," 161–75.

13. Kuznesof, *Household Economy*, 162, 169, 181. See Kuznesof's comments on single female household headship in the work of Donald Ramos, Silvia Arrom, and Kathleen Waldron (162, n. 15). Elsewhere, Kuznesof observes that female-headed households have not "typically been portrayed as exceeding 10 percent to 15 percent of total households in a comparable historical period elsewhere" ("Household and Family Studies," 305–37, 309).

14. In her study of the women of Mexico City, Silvia Arrom has concluded that "Women of higher classes were less likely to be wives and mothers, and more likely to head their own households than women of the lower classes" (*The Women of Mexico City, 1790–1857*, 134–37). However, Kuznesof has noted that Arrom's sample from the Mexico City census of 1811 is perhaps too small to be convincing, and I agree ("Household and Family Studies," 305–37, 310–12).

15. Matos suggests that the "high incidence of single-headed households" might be the result of Church and state efforts to "eradicate concubinage around mid-century" ("Economy, Society and Urban Life," 182). It is prudent to assume that such efforts did influence some people, but the degree of influence remains to be established. Other factors seem more significant. For the

This conclusion is also implied by free colored marital patterns. Recent studies have suggested a direct link between favorable economic conditions and marital rates, with the more affluent marrying at a higher rate than the less affluent, with whites marrying at a higher rate than did free people of color.[16] In the city of San Juan, a moderately higher percentage of white males, ages 15–49, were married than free colored males in three barrios, with the differential ranging from 2.2 percent in the barrio of San Francisco in 1833 to 5.2 percent in the first *trozo* of Santo Domingo in 1846 (Table 5.4). (There were very few consensual unions enumerated in the four San Juan barrio censuses.) In the barrio of San Juan in 1828, a slightly higher percentage of free colored males were married than were whites. In this barrio of high real estate values and residential prestige, it may have been that those free colored males who were able to survive the demands of the local economy found themselves high enough on the scale of economic achievement to be able to marry and raise a family or perhaps to think such a familial arrangement socially and culturally desirable.

The relationship between economics (and race) and marriage is further suggested by the marital rates among females in the four barrios. In each instance, a remarkably larger proportion of white females were married than were free colored females (Table 5.5 and Figure 5.1). Whether this was the consequence of fewer males or fewer males economically well off enough to marry and support a family, the cause must have been economic.[17]

Are there clues to the nature and meaning of Puerto Rican family and household formation, and marital patterns, in the racial

---

Church's attitude regarding concubinage, see María T. Barceló Miller, "De la polilla a la virtud: Visión sobre la mujer de la Iglesia jeráquica de Puerto Rico," in Yamila Azize Vargas, ed., *la mujer en Puerto Rico* (Río Piedras, P.R., 1987), 50–88.

16. See Swann, *Tierra Adentro*, 225–36.

17. Furthermore, in all four barrios a greater percentage of the white female population was widowed, suggesting perhaps that relatively more white women were better provided for than their free colored counterparts and better able to maintain their widowed status. It is likely that some spinsters and single women with children declared themselves to be widows within both races. See the comments in Arrom, *Women of Mexico City*, 111–21.

Table 5.4. Marital Status (in Percent) by Race and Sex among Those Age
15–49 in Four San Juan Barrios, 1823–1846

	Married		Single		Widowed	
	%	N	%	N	%	N
1823						
White						
Female	31.8	63	55.6	110	12.6	51
Male	33.3	55	63.6	105	3.0	5
Free Colored						
Female	20.7	69	72.7	242	6.6	22
Male	29.2	43	68.8	99	1.4	2
1828						
White						
Female	31.7	93	54.9	161	13.3	39
Male	29.1	57	68.9	135	2.0	4
Free Colored						
Female	22.0	38	71.1	123	6.9	12
Male	29.9	29	67.0	65	3.1	3
1833						
White						
Female	30.1	128	61.4	261	8.5	36
Male	25.4	106	72.4	304	1.9	8
Free Colored						
Female	15.1	54	78.2	279	6.7	24
Male	23.2	47	76.4	155	0.5	1
1846						
White						
Female	28.8	61	61.8	131	9.4	20
Male	36.1	48	60.2	80	3.8	5
Free Colored						
Female	14.8	25	78.7	133	6.5	11
Male	30.9	21	63.2	43	5.9	4

Note: The horizontal columns do not in each instance total 100 percent due to rounding.

Table 5.5. Percent Married among White and Free Colored Females
Age 15–49 in Four San Juan Barrios, 1823–1846

	White	Free Colored
1823	31.8	20.7
1828	31.7	22.0
1833	30.1	15.1
1846	28.8	14.8

history of the United States? The significance of single female–headed households in the United States remains fairly opaque after several decades of often vitriolic debate.[18] However, as a result of analyses of the 1990 United States Census and the recent publication of Andrew Billingsley's *Climbing Jacob's Ladder: The Enduring Legacy of African-American Families* and Andrew Hacker's *Two Nations: Black and White, Separate, Hostile, Unequal,* the discussion has become much more reasoned and informed.

All rigorous studies of the African-American experience in slavery and freedom now recognize that we know far too little about the diversity of the African heritage and the manner in which that heritage survives. The need for further study and understanding applies also and perhaps even more so to Puerto Rico. With regard to the United States, several things are now patently clear. Slavery did not entirely destroy the slave family, but in any event after the Civil War the free colored population lived overwhelmingly in families with two parents present. The single female–headed family that prevails today among African-Americans clearly was not a legacy of slavery. In 1890, 80 percent of African-American families with children were two-parent families. After seventy years, this family structure had fallen by only 2 percent.[19] However, by 1990

18. See, for instance, Lee Rainwater and William L. Yancey, eds., *The Moynihan Report and the Politics of Controversy* (Cambridge, Mass., 1967), 39–124.

19. Billingsley, *Climbing Jacob's Ladder,* 36.

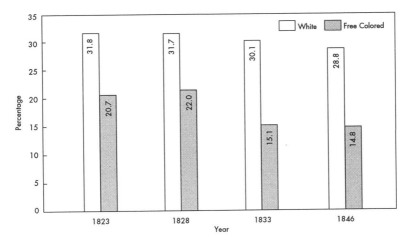

Figure 5.1. Married White and Free Colored Females, Ages 15–49, 1823–1846

only 39 percent of African-American families with children were headed by married or common law couples.[20] To put it another way, in 1950, 17.2 percent of African-American households were headed by women, but in 1991 the figure was 58.0 percent (as compared to 17.9 percent among whites).[21]

Why this precipitous decline in the African-American family, and what are its implications? As Billingsley has observed, scholars find "that the single-parent family is not generated from within African-American culture or values but from forces in the wider society, largely beyond their immediate control."[22] William Cross argues that "the nemesis of black life is not the black family, it is the black struggle with unemployment, racism, and a containment-oriented welfare system."[23] Except for the comment about welfare (since no such system existed in Puerto Rico, and in fact the opposite was true—commercial capitalism was unsupportive

20. Ibid.
21. Hacker, *Two Nations*, 68.
22. Billingsley, 35.
23. Quoted in ibid.

and unforgiving in its realities), essentially the same was true for nineteenth-century Puerto Rico, where limited economic opportunity and racial prejudice undermined the basic structure of the free colored family.[24]

Was the female-headed, single-parent family in Puerto Rico dysfunctional? Certainly most people would agree that having a male role model is helpful in the socialization of children, especially male children, but this view need not be stretched across cultures and time. In the first place, Andrew Cherlin contends that the central problem with the female, single-parent African-American family "is not the lack of a male presence but the lack of a male income."[25] This problem crosses cultures and time without strain.

24. In coding the censuses he studied, Félix Matos was tempted to view the San Juan families through the filter of modern feminist literature, but for purposes of comparability he chose—wisely, I believe—to view the family in the traditional manner, which holds that it was normal and desirable for a family to consist of a husband, wife, and their children, as well perhaps as other relatives. See Matos, "Economy, Society and Urban Life," 134–35. There is much attractive in the feminist view that the family should be considered in a broad historical context and as an element of kinship rather than an isolated demographic unit of study. However, to consider the single female–headed family a counterhegemonic response to elite mores is another matter indeed. This is not the place for me to mount a concerted criticism of such romantic intellectualism, but I will note that it is unlikely that poor women elected to impoverish themselves further by maintaining marital or consensual partner–free households in order to make a statement to or to thwart the elite. One may well wonder about consciousness of decision and strategy in the absence of alternatives.

A more productive approach would be to examine the single-parent female-headed household as a vestige of African heritage, as suggested by Sidney W. Mintz and Richard Price in *The Birth of African-American Culture: An Anthropological Perspective* (Boston, Mass., 1992), 78–79.

25. Quoted in Hacker, *Two Nations*, 73. The question of whether the single-parent female-headed African-American family in the United States is dysfunctional is, of course, extremely controversial. With regard to Puerto Rico, there is one avenue of inquiry that has not been touched upon but which is of great importance. In 1955, Leon Drusine discussed the Puerto Rican family in terms of the "patriarchal, authoritarian pattern of the Spanish Family [that] still largely exists in Puerto Rico, with the despotic father-husband relationship the dominant island pattern" ("Some Factors in Anti-Negro Prejudice among Puerto Rican Boys in New York City" [Ph.D. diss., New York University, 1955], 20, 20–23). When the father is absent, what becomes of traditional child rearing? We

Whatever the totality of problems inherent in the Puerto Rican single-parent, female-headed family, clearly the widespread absence of a male income was vexatious. Writing of female-headed Puerto Rican families in the modern period, Clara E. Rodríguez argues, "There is no historical evidence that sustains any generalization other than that life becomes economically difficult for a woman alone with children."[26] That is about as cogently as this issue has ever been put.[27]

In the second place, it is now widely accepted that the African-American family was more broadly based than statistics about nuclear families would indicate. The African-American family exists beyond the confines of the nuclear structure through what Billingsley characterizes as "the relationship of appropriation." That is, African-Americans form families "simply by deciding to live and act toward each other as family."[28] This includes multigenerational

---

need to know much more about those young boys (and I suspect, girls) who came to maturity in families without a resident male authoritarian figurehead, but here our historical methodologies fail us.

Because I am interested in the family structure for what it tells us about economic performance and racial prejudice, I have studied the family according to traditional methods. However, there is a growing trend among Latin Americanists, under the strong influence of Robert McCaa, to study families according to individual level measures. In this case, rather than calculating how many children each family had on average, the historian would ask, How many children were exposed to the phenomenon of single-headed families? See the articles in the McCaa-edited issue of the *Journal of Family History* 16:3 (1991) and Steven Ruggles, *Prolonged Connections: The Rise of the Extended Family in Nineteenth-Century England and America* (Madison, Wis., 1987).

26. Rodríguez, *Puerto Ricans*, 38.

27. I would like to add to her comment, however, by discussing a headline on the front page of the *New York Times* of June 6, 1994: "Black Household Income Leads Whites' in Queens." This was a rather stunning announcement about conclusions to be drawn from the 1990 United States Census. The *Times* asked, "How did blacks surpass whites in median income?" The answer: "They earned it. In black households both husband and wife were more likely to have jobs than in white households, and they worked longer hours, as well. And sons and daughters in black households were more likely to remain at home and help support the family, rather than leave and live on their own."

28. Billingsley, *Climbing Jacob's Ladder*, 31. See also Hacker, *Two Nations*, 78–79.

families living under one roof, or, significantly, spread out within a city or even farther away, and it includes what are referred to as "fictive kin," people who act and are accepted as relatives. Scholars of Spanish America have long written about extended families and the ameliorative benefits of the system of *compadrazgo,* or "god-parenthood," but are only now discerning the spatial nature of family and family life. Some single-parent females may have had real and fictive kin and support within their immediate neighborhoods and beyond.[29] It has not been possible to determine this for the city of San Juan, but the extended family has been such a commonplace among Puerto Ricans in the United States and in the island during the twentieth century that there is a strong likelihood that it was so also during the nineteenth century. As Emelicia Mizio has observed, "The Puerto Rican family is, in contrast to the American, an extended family; intimate relationships with the kinship system are of high value and a source of pride and security."[30]

However, the main concern here is not whether the single-parent, female-headed family was in many and perhaps most cases the result of limited economic success among free colored males—which is a conclusion of this book—but whether this was the result of a long history of racial prejudice. There appears to be no way to avoid the conclusion that, at bottom, racial prejudice played a heavy hand in free colored economic performance and therefore family structure. An attempt to give further credence to this conclusion will be made in the following chapter.

29. Of course, for some, the presence of a helpful family network might have meant dissipated capital and retarded economic advancement. This would have been especially deleterious at the lower and middle socioeconomic levels, where most free people of color were situated.

30. Emelicia Mizio, "Impact of External Systems on the Puerto Rican Family," *Social Casework* 55:2 (Feb. 1974), 77. See also Mills, Senior, and Goldsen, *The Puerto Rican Journey,* 8, and Felix Padilla, *Puerto Rican Chicago,* 72–78.

6. Paths of Opportunity?

THE MODERN WESTERN WORLD has provided many paths of opportunity for social and economic advancement. Prominent among them have been education, the military, crafts, and commerce. This chapter explores these opportunities for free people of color in nineteenth-century Puerto Rico.

EDUCATION

It is generally agreed that education provides a means for upward socioeconomic mobility, that the school is an institution for personal betterment. Even Harvey J. Graff, who has argued persuasively that literacy may not do what educators and social reformers have long claimed, recognizes that "literacy could be important, of course, to individual men and women as well as to their society."[1] In his study of four nineteenth-century Canadian cities, he found that although some occupations "may not always have required literacy . . . literacy facilitated opportunities for entry to" them.[2] Of course, discussions about poverty today emphasize education and jobs as the way out of that poverty. The question is, to what degree did racial prejudice limit educational and job opportunities?

Throughout Spanish America educational opportunities for free

---

1. Harvey J. Graff, *The Literacy Myth: Literacy and Social Structure in the Nineteenth-Century City* (New York, 1979), xviii, 115.
2. Ibid., 115.

people of color were invidiously circumscribed, perhaps most dramatically, as we have seen, in their exclusion from pursuing university degrees. Although there was no university in Puerto Rico, some island youth studied at the university in nearby Santo Domingo, as well as at those in Venezuela and Mexico.[3] It appears that it was not until nearly the middle of the nineteenth century that substantial numbers of Puerto Ricans began to send their sons to Europe for their education. One of them was Ramón Emeterio Betances, born in the town of Cabo Rojo in 1827 to ostensibly white parents. Betances, who would later become a leader of the Puerto Rican independence movement, studied for his bachelor's degree in Toulouse, France, and received his degree in medicine in Paris in 1855. Stimulated by the France of 1848 and the Puerto Rico of the same year, the one which saw the decree against the African race, Betances became perhaps the first "white" Puerto Rican of African descent, as Ada Suárez Díaz has observed, to have a clear sense of what he was in racial terms, the first "to have a consciousness of his *negritud*."[4] It may be that other Puerto Rican free people of color had become physicians and lawyers and practiced in the island, as occurred in Cuba, but perhaps as in Cuba they were counted as white.[5]

However, it was really at the other end of the educational continuum that access was most important to both free people of color and whites. The attainment of even a rudimentary education—the basic skills of reading, writing, and arithmetic—might open economic opportunity at the bottom reaches of the socioeconomic structure. It was at this level that most of the island's population existed, and it was here that education may have been most important. Simple skills, easily taken for granted, were those that might

3. See Antonio C. Mendoza, *Historia de la educación en Puerto Rico (1512–1826)* (Washington, D.C., 1937), 161–75.

4. Ada Suárez Díaz, *El Doctor Ramón Emeterio Betances y la abolición de la esclavitud* (2d ed.; San Juan, 1980), 1–2, 9. The free colored son of Don Jacabo Decastro, of Mayagüez, studied in Germany (Díaz Soler, *Historia de la esclavitud negra*, 250).

5. Klein, *Slavery in the Americas*, 204–5.

allow one to become a clerk in a store or to enter the lower bureaucracy. During the first half of the nineteenth century, primary education in Puerto Rico was provided by the Church, private schools, private tutors, and public schools.[6] There appears to have been no concerted effort on the part of the government or of white society in general either to exclude free people of color from an elementary education or to ensure access to such education.[7] There were no African churches, as in the United States for instance, to provide elementary education for free people of color,[8] nor was there anything comparable to the Colonial Charity School, established in Barbados in 1818 for the education of nonwhites who were not capable of paying for their education.[9]

The first effective attempt to create a system of public primary education in Puerto Rico may have occurred in 1805, when it was decreed that every district (*partido*) in the island must establish

6. Juan José Osuna, *A History of Education in Puerto Rico* (Río Piedras, P.R., 1949), 43. On the presence of the Church in education, see Mendoza, *Historia de la educación, passim.* I would be very surprised to learn that the Church-run schools excluded free colored youth from primary studies. This seems most unlikely because there was enough affluence among free people of color for a considerable number of parents to have sustained children as full-time students at the secondary level. It remains to be seen whether these children had access to the Church's secondary education.

One of San Juan's first schools, established during the 1820s, was founded by Celestina Cordero, a woman of color (Acosta-Belén, ed., *The Puerto Rican Woman*, 5). Cordero's brother, Rafael, was a well-known artisan and teacher, who maintained his shop and school of primary letters in his house on the third block (*manzana*) of Calle la Luna in the barrio of Santa Bárbara. In 1833 the house bore the number 7 (Cordero was then enumerated as an unmarried Negro), but today it bears the number 315 and is memorialized by a handsome plaque.

7. There was opposition to education for free people of color in some places. See, for instance, Berlin, *Slaves Without Masters,* 75–78; Curry, *The Free Black,* 152; Jackson, *Free Negro Labor,* 19–21; Bowser, *The African Slave,* 311–13.

8. Berlin, *Slaves Without Masters,* 303–6.

9. Handler, *The Unappropriated People,* 173. The absence of separate schools for free colored youth is an indication that they may have been welcome in the existing schools. See Mendoza's comments on the earlier period (*Historia de la educación,* 43–44).

a school teacher charged with educating the local youth—boys and girls—in reading, writing, counting, and religious doctrine and dogma.[10] Nothing was said about racial exclusion, and it has not been possible to determine whether free colored children attended any of the schools that might have been founded. San Juan already had a public primary school, and several months prior to the 1805 decree the town council advertised for a new teacher. One of the requirements was purity of blood.[11] However, it is not clear whether this requirement also applied to students. At one point during the early nineteenth century in the town of Bayamón, 15 students, all boys, studied with Don Antonio Aguayo. They were all white.[12] In 1842, the public school of the town of Aguada had 32 students, again all boys. In one official document their race was not stated, but they all bore the honorific *don*.[13] Fifty-four students attended the public school of the town of Pepino between November 1839 and the end of August 1842. In one document that did not indicate race, 7 were labeled as poor.[14] However, there appear to have been 2 free boys of color among the 15 male students in the public school of the town of Las Piedras in 1848.[15]

10. AGPR, Gobernadores, Instrucción Pública, leg. 728, año de 1805, caja 326, decreto no. 33, September 17. In 1770, Puerto Rico was divided into twenty-two districts, each required to establish a primary school and to educate the island's youth, regardless of color, in basic skills and catechism, but there is no evidence that the schools ever functioned (Osuna, *A History of Education*, 17–18).

11. *ACSJ*, 1803–1809, 149–50. Rosa M. Torruellas has noted that "the explicit policy of the most prestigious secondary school in Puerto Rico, the Seminario Conciliar founded in 1832, was to accept students of Spanish origin only" ("Learning in Three Private Schools in Puerto Rico," 42).

12. AGPR, Gobernadores, Instrucción (Escuelas), 1811–1826, caja 327, entry 223. There were separate schools for girls.

13. Ibid., 1827–1849, caja 328, entry 223; Comisión de Instrucción Primaria, 1842.

14. Ibid.

15. Ibid., Comisión de Instrucción Pública, 1848. Thirteen of the boys were white and bore the honorific. The two without the *don* were almost certainly pardos: they were labeled "P," but there is a slight chance that this meant *pobre* (poor).

It is more than likely that some free colored boys and girls were educated in the island's public schools. In 1854, Governor Norzagary reported to Spain his favorable impression of the island's public education. Each school, he noted, enrolled a fixed number of poor children, so that the lack of means would not impede their receiving an education.[16] Puerto Rico did not actually have its own organic educational law until 1865. This law provided for the creation of special schools for the island's free colored children.[17]

Regardless of where and when they were educated, it is certain that many of Puerto Rico's free people of color did acquire at least a rudimentary education. The standard of measurement employed to determine whether an individual was capable of reading and writing in nineteenth-century Puerto Rico is unknown. Furthermore, there doubtless was inaccuracy in both estimation of literacy and in reporting the numbers.[18] However, any inaccuracies more than likely affected the numbers for whites and free people of color similarly. Interestingly, literacy figures were compiled by census enumerators for the 5th Department (undated but probably the 1840s or 1850s) and for the city of Ponce in 1860. As can be seen in Table 6.1, by modern expectations, only a small percentage of the free colored population and the white females were literate. It seems safe to surmise that white males were perhaps modestly more literate than white females, but this may not have been the case. Yet, what seems remarkable is that so many people of both races had acquired some degree of literacy. More than 4,000 white

16. AGPR, Gobernadores, caja 342; "Diario del Gobernador Norzagary," in *Anales de investigación histórica*, 6:1 (Enero-Junio, 1979), 70–132.

17. Osuna, *A History of Education*, 54–55. The Spanish education law of 1834 did apply, but it was not designed with Puerto Rico in mind. A special law of 1842 for Cuba and Puerto Rico was not put into effect but became the basis of the 1865 law (ibid., 38–40). In 1856, a proposal was made by Master cabinetmaker Don Carlos Lassalle for the establishment of a school for artisans, that is, a school for the training of children in the crafts and in morality. If indeed the school finally functioned, it would unavoidably have educated free colored children, since so many of the artisans themselves were free colored.

18. See ibid., 39–40, on the problem of accuracy in reporting educational data.

Table 6.1. Literacy Rates in Puerto Rico's 5th Department
(Eight Years Old and Older)

Town or District	Population	% Read and Write	% Read Only
Free Colored Males			
Ponce	6,935	9.6	4.9
Adjuntas	1,010	6.3	4.3
Aibonito	469	7.9	22.0
Barranquitas	475	10.3	6.1
Barros	906	4.9	11.3
Coamo	2,016	3.4	1.9
Guayanilla	1,834	2.5	0.93
Juana Díaz	563	13.0	8.0
Peñuelas	2,042	18.7	2.0
Santa Isabel	688	3.8	0.87
Yauco	5,314	10.5	7.5
Free Colored Females			
Ponce	7,210	2.9	4.4
Adjuntas	1,734	2.5	2.2
Aibonito	345	10.1	11.6
Barranquitas	1,467	13.4	3.5
Barros	841	10.3	9.6
Coamo	1,949	2.0	1.5
Guayanilla	1,581	6.8	2.7
Juana Díaz	571	12.4	7.7
Peñuelas	1,956	14.6	1.3
Santa Isabel	542	5.5	4.1
Yauco	3,902	8.6	10.7
White Females			
Ponce	7,173	25.5	5.5
Adjuntas	2,345	9.1	4.4
Aibonito	632	8.2	19.1
Barranquitas	1,786	9.0	12.4
Barros	1,257	4.1	6.8

(Table 6.1. continued)

Town or District	Population	% Read and Write	% Read Only
Coamo	885	7.9	2.5
Guayanilla	1,033	20.9	4.9
Juana Díaz	6,575	11.5	7.3
Peñuelas	1,307	18.7	3.4
Santa Isabel	222	33.0	18.0
Yauco	2,140	32.3	35.8

Note: No data for white males were located. The population figures in the table include those eight years and older. The census categorizes ages 0–1 and 1–7, but these cohorts were deleted in my calculations because most could not have been literate. However, a few may have been considered literate, which would reduce the calculated rates slightly.
Source: AGPR, Gobernadores, Censo y Riqueza, caja 15, census of the 5th Department.

females, according to this census, knew how to read and write, and more than 2,000 others knew how to read only. To the extent that these figures are accurate and meaningful, and some skepticism is in order, there must have been much private schooling and tutoring in the 5th Department.[19] Although it is not surprising that more white females were literate than either male or female free people of color, it is nonetheless impressive that many free people of color were literate. More than 2,000 free colored males knew how to read

19. There were 1,132 foreigners and transients in the 5th Department, and perhaps they added to the literacy of both races. However, there were only 2 in Aibonito; 1 in Barranquitas; 24 in Barros; and 68 in Juana Díaz (16 free coloreds and 52 whites). José L. Vásquez Calzada has noted a total matriculation of only 1,663 students in the island's schools in 1858. In that year there were 215,900 people in Puerto Rico aged 5–19, meaning that only 0.8 percent of the school-aged population was then matriculated (*La población de Puerto Rico*, 70–71). By 1864, there supposedly were 74 public schools for boys and 48 for girls in the island with several thousand students in attendance, the majority of each sex being "poor." The school census of that year states that the city of San Juan had 29 public and 4 private schools, educating 650 boys and girls, 397 of them "poor" (Osuna, *A History of Education*, 612).

and write, and more than a thousand more knew how to read only. Perhaps even more surprising, more than 1,400 free colored females knew how to read and write, and more than a thousand others knew how to read only. Apparently, many free colored parents were determined to have their children—not excluding girls—educated.

In fact, it is clear that free colored females were not routinely deprived an education in favor of males (Table 6.1). In 5 out of the 11 towns or districts in the 5th Department, a greater percentage of free colored females knew how to read and write than did males. In a sixth town, Juana Díaz, the difference in the percentages was insignificant.

Even had one expected a greater percentage of white females to be literate than either free colored sex, attesting to the privileged position of whites in this society of racial restriction, it is nonetheless somewhat striking that in 7 of the 11 towns and districts, a greater percentage of white females knew how to read and write than did free colored males, and in the case of Aibonito and Peñuelas the two were nearly equal. Typical of the anomalous nature of Puerto Rican racial prejudice, however, in four cases—Aibonito, Barranquitas, Barros, and Juana Díaz—a larger percentage of free colored females knew how to read and write than did white females.

It may be assumed that it was at least as easy for free people of color to acquire literacy in the island's larger cities, especially, as shall be suggested, because most free colored youth probably received their educations through the craft apprentice system. Indicative of this is the considerable degree to which free people of color in Puerto Rico's "second" city, Ponce, were literate in 1860. Table 6.2 demonstrates the incidence of literacy, in this case the ability to read *or* write, among Puerto Rican males in three of Ponce's five barrios, grouped by occupational category. It is not surprising that white males dominated the nonproductive and professional ranks or that almost everyone in these two categories knew how to read or write. It is interesting, however, that almost all of the free people of color in these two occupational categories knew how to read or write. That white males so dominated the commercial occupations is something to be discussed shortly. In

Table 6.2. Literacy among Ponce Males in 1860, Barrios 2, 4, and 5

Nonmanual Workers	White N*	White R/W	Free Colored N	Free Colored R/W	Slave N	Slave R/W
Nonproductive†	35	33	2	1	0	0
Professional	55	53	8	7	0	0
Commercial	206	198	28	12	7	2
Manual Workers	N	R/W	N	R/W	N	R/W
Skilled Workers	97	65	196	87	23	2
Unskilled Workers	22	6	103	11	77	0
Totals	414	355	337	118	107	4

Literacy Rate: White = 85.7%   Free Colored = 35.0%   Slave = 3.7%

Others	N	R/W	N	R/W	N	R/W
Students	134	28	8	5	0	0
Preparing for Clergy	0	0	2	2	0	0
Apprentice	2	1	11	4	1	0
Carpentry Apprentice	0	0	2	2	0	0
Ynquilino	1	1	1	1	1	1

*N = number; R/W = those who could read or write or both.
†This category includes the clergy and Church officials, royal bureaucracy, military, and municipal bureaucracies.
Source: Archivo Municipal de Ponce, caja 53-B, Padrón nominal del . . . año de 1860.

this category—commercial occupations—we see the greatest disparity in literacy achievement between whites and free people of color. More than 96 percent of the white males in the commercial occupations had acquired some degree of literacy, whereas only about 43 percent of the free coloreds had done so. Interestingly, seven slaves were commercially occupied, and two of them knew how to read or write. The category of skilled worker is especially informative regarding literacy.

As shall be seen, it is not unexpected that free people of color would predominate in the skilled trades, but it is unexpected that so many of them achieved some degree of literacy. More than 44 percent of the free colored male skilled workers knew how to read or write, and nearly 68 percent of their white counterparts did. Although some skilled workers, white or free colored, could function in a state of illiteracy, these figures suggest that knowing how to read or write was at least helpful, and perhaps necessary, especially in those trades in which shopkeeping played a significant role. Furthermore, since almost all of the students in these three barrios were white, it seems likely that most of the literate free colored skilled workers received a substantial part of their education primarily through the apprenticeship system. That a greater percentage of white skilled workers knew how to read or write than free colored is further testament to the advantage of having been white in Puerto Rico.

It is clear that some degree of education leading at least to a rudimentary literacy was available to Puerto Rico's free colored population of both sexes, although seemingly not to the extent that it was available to the white population.[20] If some of the island's free people of color acquired their literacy through the craft apprenticeship system, as appears to be the case, then it is fortunate for them that they were so predominant in certain crafts, including skilled crafts, in Ponce and in San Juan.

THE MILITARY AS OPPORTUNITY

The military has frequently been an institution of social advancement for the downtrodden.[21] This was the case in Cuba, where the

20. The U.S. Census of 1900 estimated that of a Puerto Rican population of 953,242 in 1899 only 5,045 people had more than a primary education, nearly three-quarters of whom were men (Isabel Picó de Hernández, "The History of Women's Struggle for Equality in Puerto Rico," in Acosta-Belén, ed., *The Puerto Rican Woman*, 25–37). The Puerto Rican standard of literacy during the early nineteenth century clearly was less elevated than that of the U.S. Census.

21. Such was the case with the British West India Regiments (as well as the

military also served as a vehicle for social advancement. As early as the sixteenth century free coloreds voluntarily served in the Cuban military. Later, when the volunteer militia units were formed, free coloreds were segregated into separate units, but they enjoyed the same legal rights accorded to the white militia, and they were permitted free colored officers.[22] By 1770, with the military reforms of Inspector General Alejandro O'Reilly now in place, there were 3,400 free colored militiamen out of a total of 11,667.[23] Although many free coloreds looked upon service in the militia as a vocation rather than a temporary obligation, it was perhaps the officer corps that afforded the greatest opportunity for social improvement for free colored militiamen. In 1770, one of the 3 free colored batallions (of 800 men) was composed of 34 free colored commissioned and 25 noncommissioned officers, as well as one free colored surgeon.[24]

In Puerto Rico the military also held the possibility of social

---

earlier Black Carolina Corps), established in 1795. In the West India Regiments, free coloreds became noncommissioned officers in command of whites. Furthermore, the West India Regiments provided basic education and religious training for the troops (Buckley, *Slaves in Red Coats* [New Haven, Conn., 1979], 15–25, 140–144). See also Edward Brathwaite, *The Development of Creole Society* (Oxford, 1971), 171. Goveia portrays service in the militia in the Leewards as a burden to free coloreds, a service marked by discrimination (*Slave Society in the British Leewards*, 219).

22. Klein, *Slavery in the Americas*, 211–13.

23. Ibid., 217.

24. Ibid., 216–17, 223. After 1820 the insular militia units became less important to Spain. In 1844, the free colored militia companies and batallions were abolished. They were reestablished in 1854, but were restricted in their professional capacities (ibid., 221–22). For a different and less sanguine interpretation of the possibility of social advancement for free coloreds in the Cuban military, see Allan J. Kuethe, *Cuba, 1753–1815*, (Knoxville, Tenn., 1986), 75. However, Kuethe is concerned in this regard with advancement within the larger society, whereas Klein is more interested in the possibilities of advancement even within the society of free people of color. From Kuethe's perspective there was a greater opportunity for social advancement for free coloreds in coastal New Granada, where they could purchase a captaincy in a white militia company and sometimes become legally white (ibid.; and Kuethe, "The Status of the Free Pardo in the Disciplined Militia of New Granada," *Journal of Negro History* 56:2 [1971], 105–18). On free people of color in the militia of Buenos Aires, see Andrews, *The Afro-Argentines*, 113–137.

advancement. Like Cuba, Puerto Rico was of strategic importance to Spain, and the island figured prominently in the Crown's plans to reorganize the defense of the empire following the capture of Havana by the English in 1762. It was O'Reilly who drew the plans for the reorganization of the military in Puerto Rico, just as he had done in Cuba. O'Reilly's plan of 1765 created a Disciplined Militia of 19 infantry and 5 cavalry companies. One of the 19 infantry companies was composed of free coloreds (morenos). By the end of the eighteenth century, there were 4 free colored companies in the Disciplined Militia.[25] Membership in the white units was restricted to those who could demonstrate pureness of blood.[26] However, within their own companies, free men of color could become both commissioned and noncommissioned officers.[27]

For some Puerto Rican men of color, service in the militia must have been socially satisfying. The militia companies paraded on Sundays in their fairly handsome uniforms, and they were permitted to carry firearms before this privilege became generalized among free people. The uniforms of the free colored companies were distinct from those of their white counterparts. At one point the uniforms of the free colored companies were the most colorful of all the units. A black visorless hat had the royal arms on its front and a plume of red feathers off to the left side. A long red waistcoat with yellow braid and gilded buttons was covered by a long blue outer coat with red cuffs and gilded buttons at the front. Beneath was a white collar and a black tie. The pants were white and the leggings black.[28] A matter of racial segregation, the uniform never-

25. Noel Rivera Ayala, "Las Milicias Disciplinadas Puertorriqueñas," 34–36; Carlos Fernando Chardón, Reseña histórica del origin y desarrollo de las Milicias Disciplinadas Puertorriqueñas bajo el régimen Español (1511–1898) (San Juan, 1978), 18–20, 25. In 1830, there were four free colored companies (Córdova, Memorias geográficas, históricas . . . de Puerto Rico, II, 402).

26. Rivera Ayala, "Las Milicias Disciplinadas," 252; Flinter, An Account of the Present State . . . of Puerto Rico, 103. There is a possibility that some ostensibly white units eventually contained free colored soldiers (Rivera Ayala, 255).

27. Rivera Ayala, "Las Milicias Disciplinadas," 51.

28. Chardón, Reseña histórica de . . . las Milicias Disciplinadas, 22 and

theless must have been appealing. More importantly, perhaps, the armaments of the white and free colored infantry units were the same—musket, bayonet, and short saber.[29] By forming the free colored men into units of the Disciplined Militia and arming them just as it did the whites, the Crown was acknowledging the importance it placed on the role the free coloreds were expected to play in the island's defense. In so doing, the Crown knowingly conveyed a status upon the free people of color that could not have been lost on its recipients. Furthermore, militiamen were entitled to the military *fuero* in both civil and criminal matters, meaning that they were not subject to the local jurisdiction of the town councils, those symbols of the white establishment. In this regard also, free people of color were treated as equal with whites.

Yet, for all of its obvious attractions and benefits, the military was at bottom an institution of racial restriction. Beyond the fundamental policy of segregation, the commissioned officers of the free colored militia companies almost always appear to have been white. In Puerto Rico, all officers were paid, and consequently were required to request permission in order to marry. Free colored as well as white officers, commissioned and noncommissioned, were permitted to marry only daughters of officers or of fathers of noble and illustrious origin,[30] not a likely prospect for the free colored. To the extent that this restriction was implemented in Puerto Rico, it could not have encouraged free colored men to become officers in the militia.

There were also detractions of a more mundane nature. Those

---

plate 3. Earlier, during the 1780s, the uniform was different. See Archivo General de las Indias, sección Audiencia de Santo Domingo, leg. 2360, Compañias Sueltas de Milicias Disciplinadas de Ynfanteria y Cavalleria de la Ysla de San Juan de Puerto Rico, June 6, 1784 (microfilm, Centro de Investigaciones Históricas, University of Puerto Rico).

29. Ibid.

30. Rivera Ayala, "Las Milicias Disciplinadas," 54–55. This regulation was continued in the plans of military reorganization issued in 1826 and 1846 (ibid., 140–48, 211). The 1826 restriction was somewhat softened, but the officer's prospective father-in-law had to be of pure blood. The regulation of 1846 essentially repeated that of 1826 (ibid.).

militiamen who owned or worked in stores or shops customarily open on Sunday, the day of militia parading and training, might have found military service inconvenient or even burdensome.[31] On the other hand, militia service in Puerto Rico did not offer the benefits of extended occupation, and no free men of color were among the permanently garrisoned troops on the island.

Indeed, on balance, the Puerto Rican militia did not have a compelling attraction for free men of color. Desertions were commonplace among both whites and free coloreds.[32] Absence from drills was not uncommon either.[33] The Puerto Rican militia had its one moment of glory in 1797, when an English attack against the island was repulsed, and the free colored militiamen played a role in this defense of the island.[34] Once that moment of heroic excitement was gone, however, service in the militia became languorous. It eventually became difficult for the free colored militia units to fill their ranks. In 1842, for example, each of the 4 free colored infantry companies was required to consist of 100 men. The 1st company, that of San Juan, had only 72 men on October 1. The 2nd company, of the town of Cangrejos, could muster less than half its required complement. The 3rd company, Bayamón, could fill only 31 of its required 100 positions. Similarly, the 4th company, Vega Baja, was in dismal condition: it was missing 64 men.[35]

Altogether, service in the militia, while conveying some status and privilege, cannot be considered a means of social or economic advancement for Puerto Rico's free people of color.

31. As occurred in Mexico. See, for example, Kinsbruner, *Petty Capitalism*, 85–86.

32. See, for instance, *La Gaceta*, January 18, 1842, January 22, 1842, and February 10, 1842; and AGPR, Gobernadores, Military Affairs, Conducta-Donativos, caja 232, entries 138–43.

33. See, for instance, AGPR, Gobernadores, Militar (Asuntos) 1840–1843, caja 242, leg. 2166, entry 151.

34. Rivera Ayala, "Las Milicias Disciplinadas," 78–84; Juan Manuel Zapatero, "De la Batalla del Caribe: El ultimo ataque Inglés a Puerto Rico (17 de Abril a 1 de Mayo de 1797)," *Historia Militar*, 3 (1959), 91–134.

35. AGPR, Gobernadores, Military Affairs, Artilleria–Cuerpo de Morenos, caja 229, leg. 2161, entries 132–36, Cuerpo de Morenos Leales, Milicianos de Infantería.

CRAFTS AND COMMERCE

In many parts of the Americas free people of color were well represented in both skilled and unskilled occupations, and Puerto Rico was no exception. Examples of this for San Juan have already been noted, but unfortunately the documents do not permit a detailed analysis of the place and activities of that city's free people of color in the crafts or other occupations. Prior to 1767 there were eight guilds in San Juan, but these functioned without the traditional supervision of the town council or any other immediate supervisory agency. In 1767, the town council exerted its authority over the guilds, and in the following year it required them to prepare rules to govern their respective organizations. Included among the guilds were the traditional occupations, such as silversmiths, masons, carpenters, and shoemakers, as well as merchants, storekeepers, and grocers.[36] On the first day of each year the town council

36. Caro Castro, *El Cabildo o régimen municipal*, II, 62–64. During the nineteenth century the Puerto Rican economy was overwhelmingly agricultural, and yet I have said nothing of the participation of the island's free people of color in that area of the economy. This is because very little has been written about the subject, and I have found very few relevant references in the archives, although I am confident that much pertinent material remains to be uncovered. José Curet has noted that in the rural barrio of Vargas, in the municipality of Ponce, 1845, some *libertos* owned small plots of land (from approximately a quarter to two acres) producing minor crops ("From Slave to *Liberto*: A Study on Slavery and its Abolition in Puerto Rico, 1840–1880" [Ph.D. diss., Columbia University, 1980], 52). In 1812, in the district of Patillas 675 whites (comprising all members of families, including squatters—in the rural regions, called *agregados*), and 1,820 free people of color (comprising all members of families, including *agregados*) sought their living through agriculture. It is interesting that the whites produced a great deal of molasses, whereas the free people of color produced practically none of this byproduct of the sugar industry. This means that to the extent that free people of color cultivated sugar they did so on small holdings, which rendered them subject to the willingness of large producers with refining capacity to accept their sugarcane for processing. Small landholders normally could not afford to maintain a refining capacity. The whites also produced more cotton (although they did not produce very much of it), more rice and more corn. However, the free people of color produced more coffee and tobacco (although neither produced very much tobacco) (AGPR,

elected one member among the silversmiths, masons, and carpenters to supervise standards of quality in their trades. The free colored silversmith, Pedro Elías, was sometimes among them.[37] Others elected were almost certainly free men of color.

Nevertheless, although the guilds existed, it does not seem that they kept or filed records. Furthermore, when the town council of San Juan sent Don Ramón Power as its deputy to the newly formed *Junta Central* in Spain in 1809, it instructed him to seek the establishment of guilds in Puerto Rico. The town council felt that many who called themselves masters of a trade operated shops that prejudiced the public more than had their shops never opened. Equally disturbing to the council, apprentices were following the bad example of their masters; many were ignorant of their trade and were of poor behavior.[38] Thus, it appears that the guilds were at best rather casual organizations. At any rate, in 1813 the liberal Cádiz *Cortes* abolished guilds in the empire. In 1815, the reestablished royal government abrogated the 1813 decree, but with the return in 1820 to the liberal Cádiz constitution of 1812 the decree abolishing guilds was reinstated.[39]

In the face of limited documentation for San Juan, we turn again to Ponce for a richer picture of occupational patterns.[40] The occupa-

Gobernadores, Censo y Riqueza, 1812–1822, caja 12, Partido de las Patillas). Agriculture was certainly an area of economic opportunity for free people of color, but there is every indication that most functioned at the subsistence level. Among the many immigrants to Puerto Rico from the Haitian Revolution were free people of color. No doubt some became prominent landowners in Puerto Rico.

37. See, for instance, the elections of 1800 through 1810 in *ACSJ*, 1798–1803, 143; 1803–1809, 30–32, 190–92, 298–301, 363–64; 1809–1810, 113–14.

38. AGPR, Gobernadores, Municipales, San Juan, 1800–1810, caja 559, entry 300, "Instrucciones dadas a Ramón Power por el Cabildo de San Juan como diputado vocal de la central, 1809, extracto."

39. For an example of abolition of guilds elsewhere, see Hector Humberto Samayoa Guevara, *Los gremios de artesanos en la Ciudad de Guatemala (1542–1821)* (Guatemala City, 1962), 81–85.

40. For a valuable discussion of the district of Ponce during the early nineteenth century, see Francisco A. Scarano, *Sugar and Slavery in Puerto Rico: The Municipality of Ponce, 1815–1849* (Madison, Wis., 1984), *passim*. On the im-

tions of practically all Puerto Rican males in 3 of Ponce's 5 urban barrios in 1860 are depicted in Table 6.3.[41] The 3 barrios held 3,973 of Ponce's 6,406 inhabitants (62 percent). As can be seen, free people of color were well represented in many of the crafts, but were decidedly underrepresented in the bureaucratic, professional, and commercial categories.[42] The Spanish caste system appears to have been quite intact in Ponce. That there was only one free person of color enumerated as a member of the military is unusual, since many free colored men were members of the militia. Most likely many more white and free colored men from barrios 2, 4, and 5 were militia soldiers. On the other hand, it is noteworthy that the free colored soldier had achieved the rank of captain.

That so few free people of color were professionals was simply the working of a long history of racial restriction. It is important that a free colored could become a scribe, but it is equally important that this was a position attainable only by white males in most instances. The same may be said about teaching, a profession of some prestige. The disparity between the numbers of white and

---

portance of Ponce during the nineteenth century, see Sepúlveda-Rivera, "San Juan de Puerto Rico," 243–46, 260–63.

41. The data are from a police census. It is to be expected that some men escaped notice. In a few instances occupations were given but not race. To gauge the representativeness of the census data, the other two barrios were examined to determine if there was occupational clustering at the barrio level, that is, whether an exceptionally large number of males involved in similar employment resided in one or two barrios rather than more or less randomly throughout the five barrios. Indeed, there was practically no clustering.

42. In grouping occupations by category for Tables 6.2 and 6.3, an attempt was made to contribute toward a standard usage for future comparative purposes. As far as seemed possible, I followed Swann, *Tierra Adentro,* 236–47, especially Table 4.18. It is not likely that anyone will be wholly successful in classifying occupations cross-culturally in the foreseeable future. An occupation of prestige in one country or region may not be one in another. To consider a barber, for instance, a professional in one place might be misleading in another, and although I might personally believe that large agriculturalists and even small farmers should be aggregated under the rubric "Commerce," I would not expect everyone to agree or want to do so. On some of the problems attendant upon such classification, see Michael B. Katz, "Occupational Classification in History," *Journal of Interdisciplinary History* 3 (1972), 63–88.

Table 6.3. Occupational Structure for Ponce Males
in Barrios 2, 4, and 5 in 1860

	White	Free Colored
NONMANUAL		
I. Nonproductive		
Bureaucracy	5	1[a]
Municipal Officers	4	0
Religious	3[b]	0
Military	21	1[c]
II. Professional		
Dentist	3	0
Physician[d]	4	0
Lawyer	3	0
Bookkeeper	4	0
Pharmacist	2	0
Scribe[e]	15	1
Notary	1	0
Painter	1	·1
Portraitist	1	0
Amanuensis	1	1
Teacher	7[f]	1
Music Teacher	0	0
Veterinerian	1	0
Musician	6	2
Barber	4	1
Architect	1	0
Land Surveyor	1	0
Totals	55	8
III. Commercial		
Merchant (*Comerciante*)	53[g]	3
Merchant (*Negociante*)	3	0
Businessman (*Comercio*)	3	3
Director	1	0 ·
Store Employee (*Dependiente*)	83	10
Employee (*Empleado*)	8	0
Salaried Employee	0	1

(Table 6.3. continued)

	White	Free Colored
Manufacturer (*Yndustrial*)	10[h]	1
Proprietor	7[i]	1
Provisioner	3	0
Grocer	1[j]	1
Large Landowner (*Hacendado*)	7	0
Landowner (*Estanciero*)	1	0
Agriculturist	11	0
Overseer (*Mayordomo*)	7	1
Small-To-Middling Farmer	8	9
Renter of Coaches or Horses	0	1
Totals	206	28

MANUAL

I. Skilled Workers

	White	Free Colored
Shoemaker	3	17
Cigar Maker	17	27
Mason	8	50
Armourer	1	0
Brazier	0	1
Cabinetmaker	2	2
Watchmaker	3	0
Tailor	21	23
Cooper	0	2
Tanner	1	0
Lathemaker	1	1
Silversmith	2	4
Smith	0	2
Hatmaker	2	0
Tobacconist	1	1
Beltmaker	1	0
Machinist	1	0
Conchero (gather or worker in shells)	1	1
Carpenter	25	53

(Table 6.3. continued)

	White	Free Colored
Baker	6	10
Buttonhole Maker	0	2[k]
Confectioner	1	0
Totals	97	196
II. Unskilled Workers		
Day Laborer	12	63
Domestic	4	23
Clothes Presser	0	1
Dressmaker (*Costurero*)	1	1
Cook	0	7
Fisherman	1	0
Servant (*Sirviente*)	1	5
Servant (*Criado*)	0	1
Sailor	1	0
Copper Worker	0	1
Totals	22	103

Population Proportions among Males: Free Colored: 715 (58.2%) and White: 514 (41.8%)

Ratios of Whites to Free Coloreds: Non-Productive: 35:2, Professional: 55.8, Skilled Workers: 96:196, and Unskilled Workers: 22:103

[a]He was a weigher of hogs; [b]Race was not given for two other priests, more than likely whites; [c]The military title in many instances was vague. This free colored man was a captain; [d]There was also a surgeon for whom no race was indicated; [e]An additional scribe was enumerated, but without racial classification; [f]Additionally, there was a white foreigner who was a teacher; [g]There was also a white foreigner who was a *comerciante*. In another instance, the racial classification of a *comerciante* was destroyed on the census page and therefore could not be read; [h]There was a white foreigner who was a manufacturer; [i]Another proprietor was a white foreigner; [j]Obviously, there were more grocers in the 3 barrios, probably in the area of 10. These must have been categorized as *comerciante*; [k]There were two additional foreign free colored buttonhole makers.
Source: Same as Table 6.2.

free colored teachers is a comment not only on the likelihood that a free colored could become a teacher, but on educational opportunities for free people of color in general. It is interesting that in the three barrios studied there were four white barbers and only one free colored.[43] Clearly, whites did not scorn this occupation to the advantage of free people of color. It is also interesting that all the barbers could either read or write. Although the arts were fairly open to free people of color in Puerto Rico, few participated. In the three Ponce barrios there was one free colored painter, two musicians, and a music teacher.

The subordinate position of the free people of color in Puerto Rican society is revealed poignantly by their participation in the commercial occupations. Of all the information presented in this book, the following is the most disturbing and the most revealing of the insidious workings of racial prejudice.

At the higher levels of the commercial hierarchy, free people of color practically did not exist. No direct legal restriction restrained them from owning retail stores or the normally more heavily capitalized and prestigious wholesale domestic or import-export operations.[44] Indeed, a few free people of color managed to enter these

43. The occupation of barber is one of considerable interest. In the South of the United States during the antebellum period, barbering was looked down upon by whites as "nigger work" and consequently became a position of opportunity for free people of color (Berlin, *Slaves Without Masters*, 235–36). In urban Virginia, free colored barbers were almost without competition from whites; many of them could read and write, and many were affluent enough to be slaveowners (Jackson, *Free Negro Labor*, 97–98, 220).

44. Free people of color were restricted from opening certain kinds of stores elsewhere in the Spanish empire. In 1604, they were prohibited from becoming master craftsmen in one trade and from opening a *tienda pública* (Konetzke, ed., *Colección de documentos*, II, 108–9). In 1757, regulations in Mexico City prohibited any person of color from owning or administering a grocery store (Kinsbruner, *Petty Capitalism*, 82); however, free people of color did own and operate grocery stores in Caracas during the late colonial period. In San Juan, Don Atlántico Vargas, pardo, was the owner of a grocery store during the 1820s. In 1851, two grocers seem to have been pardos (Kinsbruner, "The Pulperos of Caracas and San Juan," 70). The *Código de Comercio*, promulgated by the Crown for Spain in 1829 and extended to Puerto Rico in 1832, pointedly in-

ranks. Probably two forces were at work limiting free colored access to these entrepreneurial occupations. One was the effect of a racially restrictive society upon the ability of the free people of color to generate the amount of capital requisite for the larger commercial operations. A second was almost certainly the constraint placed upon free people of color by social attitudes, as occurred in New York City, where few free coloreds were employed as carters or draymen even in the absence of legal restriction.[45]

Not only were few free people of color to be counted among the merchants, few could aspire to work their way up the employee ranks. Judging by the way the terms *empleado* and *dependiente* were used in other parts of Spanish America, it is likely that the *empleados* were commercial employees of considerable importance and responsibility, more so than the *dependientes*, who were also commercial employees. The slim chance that a free person of color might become an upper-level commercial employee and then perhaps move on to ownership is suggested by the fact that none were *empleados*. Even more indicative of commercial opportunity for the free person of color is the number of *dependientes*—clerks of various description and responsibility. It is important that 10 free colored males could become clerks and that 7 of them could read or write. Certainly, there was some opportunity, but the difference in opportunity is disturbingly implicit in the number of white clerks. Why was there a more than 8 to 1 difference in favor of whites? Perhaps the pool of white literate youth was greater than the free colored, or perhaps whites, who comprised the commercial establishment, preferred to employ whites. But this can come as no shock to

cluded free people of color among those eligible to enter commerce, the only restriction being that they had to have been legally emancipated (*Legislación ultramarina*, arranged and annotated by Joaquín Rodríguez San Pedro, 5 vols. [Madrid, 1866], 5, 116). I suspect that only a few people of color might have become merchants in San Juan, although others who had previously passed into white society may have done so. In her long and competent master's thesis, "La politica del comercio: Los comerciantes de San Juan: 1837–1844" (University of Puerto Rico, 1987), Carmen Campos Esteve does not explore the issue of race.

45. Curry, *The Free Black in Urban America*, 18.

the modern reader. That all but 2 of the 83 white clerks could read or write reflected their opportunity for basic education. In barrio 3 there were 2 free colored *dependientes* (one of whom appears to have been a youthful female) and 1 merchant. However, there were 19 white *dependientes* and 29 white merchants (*comerciantes*).[46]

Racial prejudice had made it very unlikely that free people of color could take full advantage of the opportunities of commercial capitalism. Generations of prejudice and discrimination had conspired to render a "playing field" that was hardly level. It was unfair, and it was structurally unsound.

Yet, in the manner of Puerto Rico's particular kind of prejudice, there was economic opportunity for free people of color during the nineteenth century, preeminently in the skilled trades, occupations that permitted some degree of affluence and community standing. In the three Ponce barrios studied, free people of color predominated among the shoemakers, masons, and carpenters. Approximately the same number of free people of color were tailors as were whites, and since there were many of each, there is the strong indication that this was not a trade whites avoided, as they may have avoided some occupations. Importantly, there were more free colored silversmiths than white (barrio 3 had one resident free colored silversmith and one white silversmith).[47] Even if we were to guess that among the whites there were more truly master craftsmen and fewer journeymen, or more journeymen and fewer apprentices, than among the free people of color, the skilled trades still would have been occupations of opportunity for free coloreds. If indeed many free colored youth acquired all or part of their basic

46. In 1838, there were thirteen merchants of foreign origin resident in Ponce. All were white (AGPR, Gobernadores, Censo y Riqueza, caja 14, registro de estrangeros avecinados en el Partido de Ponce, año de 1838). In some commercial endeavors, free people of color may have had an advantage over whites, as with the free colored women *vendedoras* who had places on the floor of the main market in San Juan (*ACSJ*, 1798–1803, 333–36).

47. In 1838, there were four foreign silversmiths resident in urban Ponce. Three were free colored (AGPR, Gobernadores, Censo y Riqueza, caja 14, registro de estrangeros . . .).

literacy through the apprentice system, then the openness of the Puerto Rican trades to free people of color made these occupations all the more significant as institutions of opportunity.[48]

Not unexpectedly, the free people of color found opportunity, although of a different order, in the unskilled occupations. Many more of them were day laborers and domestics than were whites. Interestingly, for whatever reason, whites did work at these low-level tasks, thus placing the achievement of the free colored skilled tradesmen in clearer hierarchical perspective. It is also interesting that there were male dressmakers and cooks. In Ponce, as in San Juan, free colored females participated in the normally male trades. One was a silversmith, one a cigarmaker, another a carpenter. One female was a merchant—a *negociante*. However, most employed free colored females worked as cooks, domestics, washerwomen, or clothes pressers, as was the case in San Juan.

This was not the promise of capitalism, but the inevitable heritage of centuries of racial prejudice, even if not all Puerto Ricans would acknowledge it.

---

48. An example of a ten-year apprenticeship contract is in AGPR, PN, San Juan, caja 527, Escritura de Aprendiz, June 4, 1824, fols. 424v–26. On the place of free people of color in the crafts elsewhere, see Knight, *Slave Society in Cuba*, 94; Andrews, *The Afro-Argentines of Buenos Aires*, 40–41; Chance, *Race and Class in Colonial Oaxaca*, 164–68; Brathwaite, *The Development of Creole Society*, 172–73; Berlin, *Slaves Without Masters*, 219–20; Curry, *The Free Black in Urban America*, 15–36, 258–66. For a comparison of whites and free people of color in a section of Havana, see Jacabo de la Pezuela, *Diccionario geográfico, estadístico, histórico de la isla de Cuba*, 4 vols. (Madrid, 1863–1866), III, 351.

7. Conclusion

IT CAN COME as no surprise to anyone that in a slave society free people of color would suffer racial prejudice and generally perform less well in the economy than the dominant white society. What is remarkable about the Puerto Rican experience is the considerable degree of racial tolerance whites showed toward free people of color, as well as the notable degree of initiative and economic achievement manifested by some members of this legally and socially disadvantaged community. What is disturbing about the Puerto Rican experience is that this achievement on the part of the few points to racial prejudice as the central factor in limiting economic performance, and causes one to decry the insidious limitations such prejudice placed on the economic and indeed social development of these Puerto Ricans and, inevitably, of Puerto Rico itself.

That free people of color lived with whites, routinely lived in the same houses with them or across the street; that some became master craftsmen, even silversmiths; that some owned a house, or two or three; and that some were moderately wealthy should not becloud the fundamental perniciousness of racial prejudice in Puerto Rico. In the San Juan barrios studied, free people of color clearly were a disadvantaged group, nowhere more starkly revealed than in the demographic imbalances. When only those of normal child-rearing age, 15–49, are considered, the difference between the number of white and free colored males per one hundred white and free colored females is striking, with the free colored population resembling a community in decline, a condition further aggravated

by the relative youth of the free colored males in relation to females. There simply were not enough free colored males for free
colored females. Also, as one might have expected, in each instance
studied, free people of color manifested higher birth and death rates
than did whites.

By the nineteenth century, intrinsic racial prejudice and limited economic opportunity had become systemic. Whites in San
Juan maintained larger households than did free people of color,
although their respective nuclear families were not far apart in
size. White households were larger because whites had greater economic resources with which to support them. More revealing of the
cumulative effects of racial prejudice was the role of women in the
household. More female-headed households among free people of
color had from one to four children than occurred among whites, in
whose case the reverse was true—more white male-headed households had this number of children. More white males were capable
of heading families than were free colored males, a racially defined
economic reality. The exception occurred in the barrio of San Juan
in 1828, where apparently it was likewise difficult for white males
to have succeeded well enough in the economy to head a family.
Furthermore, in each barrio studied a larger percentage of free colored families with children present were female-headed than was
the case among whites, a strong indicator of lower economic status.

Marital patterns also reflected the workings of a long history of
racial prejudice. In each of the barrios studied, a markedly greater
percentage of white females, ages 15–49, were married than were
free colored females. The demographic imbalance and its economic
underpinnings reached deeply into family formation.

Yet, those free people of color who were able to surmount the
artificial barriers set against them were demonstrably capable of
strong social and economic performance. This is suggested especially by dwelling ownership. Few whites or free people of color
owned their own houses; however, when only those heads of households who also headed Residential Units (dwellings that may have
included other households) in the barrio of Santa Bárbara in 1823 are
considered, the degree of ownership is more impressive. In Santa
Bárbara, the barrio of lowest dwelling values, approximately the

same degree of house ownership prevailed among both whites and free people of color. When ownership is considered only within each race, a picture of achievement emerges with more than one out of every two white and free colored heads of Residential Units owning their own houses, with female and male free people of color owning houses at higher rates than their white counterparts. In fact, when ownership is considered only within each race, nearly three-fourths of all free colored heads of Residential Units owned their houses. It may be concluded that motivation was not lacking among free people of color, but rather economic means, attributable in part at least to centuries of racial deprivation.

Ironically, the free people of color of San Juan reinforced Puerto Rico's society of castes through their choice of marital partners. In the barrios studied, they largely married within their own sub-caste—those closest to white attempting to protect their place in the racial hierarchy. The people of color adopted the logic of the white establishment.

The underrepresentation of free people of color in the entrepreneurial sector of the economy, as seen in the case of Ponce, is particularly distressing. It is precisely this sector—storekeeping of all kinds, from the smallest grocery to the largest import-export operation—that would have fulfilled the promise of capitalism. It is in the realm of commerce that people of color would have acquired the skills and capital to ascend the socioeconomic structure, with ever greater capacity to draw others with them and to beat down the strictures of racial prejudice. That so few free people of color, as compared to whites, were clerks in Ponce in 1860 speaks volumes.

This was the legacy of racial prejudice to the thousands of slaves freed in the abolition of 1873—the new *libertos*. These *libertos* are currently the subject of much scholarly attention, and it remains to be seen whether their experience was significantly different from that of the free people of color during the age of slavery. What we do know is that in the twentieth century, the economic performance and social achievement of Puerto Ricans of color has been limited by racial prejudice, not the racism that has so perturbed the United States, but a prejudice and discrimination—based on race—that needs to be understood in its historical context, and confronted.

Appendix A: Historiography

Especially valuable for the United States are John H. Russell, *The Free Negro in Virginia, 1619–1865* (Baltimore, Md., 1913); Luther Porter Jackson, *Free Negro Labor and Property Holding in Virginia, 1830–1865* (2d ed.; New York, 1969); John Hope Franklin, *The Free Negro in Virginia, 1619–1865* (Baltimore, Md., 1913); 1943); Leon F. Litwack, *North of Slavery: The Negro in the Free States, 1790–1860* (Chicago, 1961); Ira Berlin, *Slaves Without Masters: The Free Negro in the Antebellum South* (New York, 1974); and Leonard P. Curry, *The Free Black in Urban America, 1800–1850: The Shadow of the Dream* (Chicago, 1981).

For the Caribbean, there are Pedro Deschamps Chapeaux, *El negro en la economía habanera del siglo XIX* (Havana, 1971); Robert L. Paquette, *Sugar Is Made with Blood: The Conspiracy of La Escalera and the Conflict between Empires over Slavery in Cuba* (Middletown, Conn., 1988); Aline Helg, *Our Rightful Share: The Afro-Cuban Struggle for Equality, 1886–1912* (Chapel Hill, N.C., 1995); Elsa V. Goveia, *Slave Society in the British Leeward Islands at the End of the Eighteenth Century* (New Haven, Conn., 1965); Edward Brathwaite, *The Development of Creole Society in Jamaica, 1770–1820* (Oxford, 1971); Philip D. Curtin, *Two Jamaicas: The Role of Ideas in a Tropical Colony* (Cambridge, Mass., 1955); Orlando Patterson, *The Sociology of Slavery: An Analysis of the Origins, Development and Structure of Negro Slave Society in Jamaica* (London, 1967); Gad J. Heuman, *Between Black And White: Race, Politics, and the Free Coloreds in Jamaica, 1792–1865* (Westport, Conn., 1981); B. W. Higman, *Slave Population and Economy in Jamaica, 1807–1834* (Cambridge, Eng., 1976); Roger Norman Buckley, *Slaves in Red Coats: The British West India Regiments, 1795–1815* (New Haven, Conn., 1979); Edward L. Cox, *Free Coloreds in the Slave Societies of St. Kitts and Grenada, 1763–1833* (Knoxville, Tenn., 1984); Jerome S. Handler, *The Unappropriated People: Freedmen in the Slave Society of Barbados* (Baltimore, Md., 1974); Herbert S. Klein, *Slavery in the Americas: A Comparative Study of Virginia and Cuba* (Chicago, 1967); Gwendolyn Midlo Hall, *Social Control in Slave Plantation Societies: A Comparison of St. Domingue and Cuba* (Baltimore, Md., 1971).

For other areas there are Carlos Larrazábal Blanco, *Los negros y la esclavitud en Santo Domingo* (Santo Domingo, 1967): A. C. De C. M. Saunders, *A Social History of Black Slaves and Freedmen in Portugal, 1441–1555* (Cambridge, Eng., 1982); A. J. R. Russell-Wood, *The Black Man in Slavery and Freedom in Colonial Brazil* (New York, 1982); William F. Sharp, *Slavery on the Spanish Frontier: The Colombian Chaco, 1680–1810* (Norman, Okla., 1967); Frederick P. Bowser, *The African Slave in Colonial Peru, 1524–1650* (Stanford, Calif., 1974); Gonzalo Aguirre Beltrán, *La población negra de México* (2d ed.; México, D.F., 1972); George Reid Andrews, *The Afro-Argentines of Buenos Aires, 1800–1900* (Madison, Wisc., 1980); Carlos M. Rama, *Los Afro-Uruguayos de Montevideo: El siglo ilustrado* (3d ed.; Montevideo, 1969); Patrick James Carroll, *Blacks in Colonial Veracruz* (Austin, Tex., 1991). Four important collections of essays are David W. Cohen and Jack P. Greene, eds., *Neither Slave nor Free: The Freedmen of African Descent in the Slave Societies of the New World* (Baltimore, Md., 1972); Robert Brent Toplin, ed., *Slavery and Race Relations in Latin America* (Westport, Conn., 1976); Stanley L. Engerman and Eugene D. Genovese, eds., *Race and Slavery in the Western Hemisphere: Quantitative Studies* (Princeton, N.J., 1975); and Magnus Mörner, ed., *Race and Class in Latin America* (New York, 1971). A recent excellent survey of the subject is in Herbert S. Klein, *African Slavery in Latin America and the Caribbean* (New York, 1986). Of interest also is Leslie B. Rout, *The African Experience in Spanish America* (Cambridge, Eng., 1976).

Appendix B: Household Coding and the Segregation Index

ALTHOUGH THE SEGREGATION INDEX is useful for purposes of comparison and generalization, like many other demographic measurements it potentially distorts historical reality because of the manner in which the heads of households are calculated. The conventional procedure is to count the first named individual in the household as its head. This method contributes to standardization of terms and renders data amenable to comparison. However, as David Robinson notes, there is room for discretion in determining the head of household, and, in fact, censuses sometimes varied considerably in how this determination was made.[1] Unfortunately, scholars typically do not indicate if, or how often, they have deviated from the standard of coding the first named in the household as its head, and one is left with the impression that deviation from convention is rare. In dealing with large numbers of people, this would almost certainly make no significant difference, but at the micro level distortions may result. For example, it is well known that men, often but not always bachelors, shared residences; and in San Juan there are many instances of bachelors—and sometimes married men or women without spouses present—sharing residences. In 1828, for example, in house number 86 in the barrio of

1. See the comment on this coding procedure in David J. Robinson, "The Analysis of Eighteenth-Century Spanish American Cities: Some Problems and Alternative Solutions" (discussion paper no. 4, Department of Geography, Syracuse University, 1975), 7 and 39, note 27. See Cook and Borah, *Essays in Population History*, 2 vols., (Berkeley, 1971), I, 136–45, on how the head of household was determined in eighteenth-century Mexico.

San Juan two white, bachelor musicians, one 23 and the other 22, rented an apartment (or a room or rooms). Conventional coding would consider these two as one household, with the 22 year old, because he is listed first, as the head of the household. This makes no good historical sense; both should be considered heads of households. To consider this bachelor household as having had only one head understates the white presence in their barrio.

Conventional coding techniques overlook many men and women, white and free colored, when such things as the Segregation Index and household ownership are calculated. By conventional coding, one block in the barrio of San Francisco had 15 white heads of households, when it would be more accurate to count as many as 30. On another block, standard coding produces 103 white heads of households when more realistically there were as many as 122. These distortions proved statistically insignificant at the barrio level when the Segregation Index was calculated both conventionally and alternatively according to a more historically accurate evaluation of each household. However, when the results of both coding methods are compared at the block level, it becomes clear that conventional coding sometimes masks a higher degree of segregation, just as it has the reverse effect on household ownership statistics, making it appear that a greater percentage of heads of households owned dwellings than actually was the case. Historians concerned about the particular in their search for the general may desire to code their censuses not only in the conventional manner but also alternatively, a time-consuming but not technically difficult task.[2]

---

2. Both methods of coding produce unexpected results. In the alternative method, there are heads of households in their early teens and even younger. However, the use of standard coding produces similar results—for instance, a seven-year-old head of household. In fact, it may be that young people of tender age managed to live alone or were placed in their residences by a benefactor. Cook and Borah have noted that clerical enumerators in late eighteenth-century Mexico sometimes counted children above the age of twelve or thirteen as heads of households (Cook and Borah, *Essays in Population History*, I, 138). A further refinement in coding procedures would be to code coresident siblings

---

according to what appears to be their actual status. When the first named sibling was somewhat older than the others, or was a person of some social or economic status, he or she might be coded the head of household. However, when the siblings were of approximately the same age, especially when they were of the same sex, each might be coded as the head of a household, unless some mitigating information in the census suggested otherwise. Who is to say that these siblings had not simply joined together as renters of individual rooms in an apartment and maintained fairly discrete "households," while sharing some common amenities, which in any event might have been the reality among some renters of separate apartments? The Cambridge Group for the History of Population and Social Structure would have coded siblings living together without the presence of a parent or other relative from an earlier generation as a *frérèche* (see Laslett, ed., *Household and Family in Past Time*, 30). The Cambridge Group considers "persons not evidently related" as members of a "no family" (ibid., 31).

Appendix C: Endogamy Ratios

ALTHOUGH THE ENDOGAMY RATE is useful, the endogamy ratio is better suited for comparison between societies. Not only does the ratio tell a great deal about any racial group measured, it also signals when a measured group is very small, as occurred among the subcastes in the present case. The endogamy ratio is the ratio of observed to expected marriages within a race or between races. The expected frequency of marriages is calculated according to the hypothetical situation of perfectly random selection among all marriage partners—a case of no racial bias in the selection of a marriage partner. Where the endogamy ratio is greater than 1.0, marital pairings within a race are indicated, whereas a ratio of less than 1.0 indicates degrees of marriage outside of one's race.[1]

As an example, we shall begin with the barrio of Santa Bárbara in 1823. Table C.1 presents the endogamy ratios for whites, free blacks (*negros libres*), and free pardos (*pardos libres*) in the barrio. The table includes all marriages of heads of households within each racial category. (As noted in the chapter, there were instances of married heads of households with no spouse enumerated, and since this is a consideration of marital pairings, these married individ-

---

1. For this discussion of endogamy I have followed Swann, *Tierra Adentro*, 174–207, especially 197–202. For a vituperative discussion of endogamy ratios and their value, see Chance and Taylor, "Estate and Class in a Colonial City: Oaxaca in 1792," 455–86; McCaa et al., "Race and Class in Colonial Latin America: A Critique," 421–33; and Chance and Taylor, "Estate and Class: A Reply," 434–42. On marriage patterns in colonial Oaxaca, see Chance, *Race and Class in Colonial Oaxaca*, 135–39.

Table C.1. Endogamy Ratios for the Barrio of Santa Bárbara, 1823

	White Males	Free Black Males	Free Pardo Males	Total
White Females	54	0	3	57
	31.7	9.9	15.4	
	1.70	0.0	0.19	
Free Black Females	1	19	4	24
	13.4	4.2	6.5	
	0.07	4.52	0.62	
Pardo Females	9	1	24	34
	18.9	5.9	9.2	
	0.48	0.17	2.61	
Total	64	20	31	115

uals do not appear in the tables.) The horizontal rows in the following four tables represent males and the vertical columns represent females. Within each cell the first number is the number of observed marriages; the second is the number of expected marriages; and the third number is the endogamy ratio (observed to expected).[2]

The very high endogamy rate for whites noted in chapter 4 is reflected in the endogamy ratio of 1.70. The very high endogamy ratios for the free colored subcastes, as seen in the table, reflect their small universes as compared to the whites, which means that a ratio of 2.0, for instance, does not necessarily indicate a higher absolute degree of endogamous marriage than a ratio of 1.0.

The high incidence of racial bias in mate selection in the barrio of San Juan in 1828 (Table C.2) is also reflected in the endogamy ratios. Here, whites produced an endogamy ratio of 1.50.[3]

2. For Tables C.1–C.4 the *chi squares* are 133.8; 147.7; 483.9; and 237.9 (all significant at .0001). The *chi squares* for the 2 x 2 tables that resulted in Table C.5 are 69.9; 95.2; 174.8; and 63.8 (all significant at .0001).
3. For the barrio of San Juan in 1828, the census enumerators used the letters M for pardo and N for moreno, as is made clear in the census summation, f. 146.

Table C.2. Endogamy Ratios for the Barrio of San Juan, 1828

	White Males	Free Pardo Males	Free Black Males	Total
White Females	69	1	0	70
	46.0	14.9	9.1	
	1.50	0.67	0.0	
Pardo Females	2	19	2	23
	15.1	4.9	3.0	
	0.13	3.88	0.67	
Free Black Females	0	3	12	15
	9.9	3.2	1.9	
	0.0	0.94	6.32	
Total	71	23	14	108

Table C.3. Endogamy Ratios for the Barrio of San Francisco, 1833

	White Males	Mulatto Males	Free Black Males	Pardo Males	Total
White Females	127	1	1	0	129
	89.0	13.3	22.4	4.2	
	1.43	0.75	0.45	0.0	
Mulatto Females	0	17	0	0	17
	11.7	1.8	3.0	0.6	
	0.0	9.44	0.0	0.0	
Free Black Females	0	1	31	1	33
	22.8	3.4	5.4	1.1	
	0.0	0.29	5.47	0.91	
Pardo Females	0	0	0	5	5
	3.5	0.5	0.9	0.2	
	0.0	0.0	0.0	25.0	
Total	127	19	32	6	184

Table C.4. Endogamy Ratios for the Barrio of Santo Domingo
(first *trozo*), 1846

	White Males	Grifo Males	Moreno Males	Free Black Males	Pardo Males	Total
White	53	0	0	0	0	53
Females	38.5	2.1	2.1	6.2	4.1	
	1.38	0.0	0.0	0.0	0.0	
Grifo	0	3	0	0	0	3
Females	2.2	0.1	0.1	0.4	0.2	
	0.0	30.0	0.0	0.0	0.0	
Moreno	1	0	2	0	0	3
Females	2.2	0.1	0.1	0.4	0.2	
	0.45	0.0	20.0	0.0	0.0	
Free Black	0	0	1	9	0	10
Females	7.3	0.4	0.4	1.2	0.8	
	0.0	0.0	2.50	7.50	0.0	
Pardo	2	0	0	0	6	8
Females	5.8	0.3	0.3	0.9	0.6	
	0.34	0.0	0.0	0.0	10.0	
Total	56	3	3	9	6	77

Table C.5. Endogamy Ratios in Four San Juan Barrios, 1823–1846

	1823	1828	1833	1846
White	1.70	1.50	1.43	1.32
Free Colored	1.87	2.77	3.24	3.23

Note: Free colored figures represent aggregate of all free colored groups.

In the barrio of San Francisco in 1833, an extreme racial preference in mate selection is manifested in the endogamy ratios, with
the whites showing a rate of 1.43 (Table C.3).

Racial bias in choosing marriage partners in the barrio of Santo
Domingo (first *trozo*) in 1846 (Table C.4) is again seen in the endogamy ratios. Among whites it was 1.38.

The degree to which whites and free people of color in the city of
San Juan married within their own races is striking (Table C.5).

Bibliography

PRIMARY SOURCES

Archives

1. Archivo General de Puerto Rico (AGPR) *Documentos de los Gobernadores de Puerto Rico*

Audiencia
Ayuntamiento de San Juan
Censo y Riqueza
Esclavos
Instrucción (Escuelas)

Instrucción Pública
Militar (Asuntos)
Military Affairs
Municipales
Tribunales

2. *Protocolos Notariales* (San Juan)
The following cajas were consulted: 256, 259, 260, 437, 438, 439, 445, 446, 451, 457, 480, 481, 482, 485, 501, 502, 527, 528, 530

3. *Archivo Histórico Diocesano, Archivo Catedral* (San Juan)

Matrimonios Pardos, 1818–1836
Libro De Bautismos, 1827–1834

Difunciones, 1826–1831
Gobierno (Asociaciones)

4. *Archivo Municipal de Ponce*

Caja 53-B

Microfilm

1. Centro de Investigaciones Históricas (CIH), Universidad de Puerto Rico (UPR), *Archivo General de las Indias*, Audiencia de Santo Domingo

2. CIH, UPR, *Archivo Histórico Nacional*, Sección: Ultramar, Gobierno de Puerto Rico

3. Family History Library, the Church of Jesus Christ of Latter-Day Saints, Parroquia Nuestra Señora De Guadalupe, Catedral (Ponce), reels 820695, 820704, 820708

Printed Documents and Contemporary Works

Abbad y Lasierra, Fray Iñigo. *Historia geográfica, civil, y política de la isla de San Juan Bautista de Puerto Rico*. Vol. 1 of Pedro Tomás de Córdova, *Memorias geográficas, históricas, económicas y estadísticas de la Isla de Puerto Rico*, 6 vols., 2d ed. San Juan, 1968 [first published 1831].

Actas del Cabildo de San Juan Bautista de Puerto Rico. San Juan, 1945–present.

Coll y Toste, Cayetano. *Boletín Histórico de Puerto Rico*, 14 vols. San Juan, 1914–1927.

Córdova, Pedro Tomás de. *Memorias geográficas, históricas, económicas y estadísticas de la Isla de Puerto Rico*, 6 vols., 2d ed. San Juan, 1968 [first published 1831].

Ferrer De Couto, José. *Los negros en sus diversos estados y condiciones. . . .* 2d ed., New York, 1864.

Flinter, Colonel George. *An Account of the Present State of the Island of Puerto Rico*. London, 1834.

Konetzke, Richard, ed. *Colección de documentos para la historia de la formación social de Hispanoamérica, 1493–1810*, 3 vols. Madrid, 1962.

Ledrú, André Pierre. *Viaje a la Isla de Puerto Rico en el año 1797*, tr. San Juan, 1971.

Legislación Ultramarina. Arranged and annotated by Joaquín Rodríguez San Pedro, 5 vols. Madrid, 1866.

Pezuela, Jacobo de la. *Diccionario geográfico, estadístico, histórico de la isla de Cuba*, 4 vols. Madrid, 1863–1866.

Ramos, Francisco, ed. *Prontuario de disposiciones oficiales, 1824–1865*. San Juan, 1866.

Schoelcher, Victor. *Colonies étrangères et Haiti*. 2 vols., Paris, 1973.

SECONDARY SOURCES

Acosta-Belén, Edna, ed. *The Puerto Rican Woman: Perspectives on Culture, History, and Society*, 2d. ed. New York, 1986.

Aguirre Beltrán, Gonzalo. *La población negra de México: Estudio etno-histórico*, 2d ed. México, D.F., 1972.

Alegría, Ricardo E. *La Fiesta de Santiago Apóstol en Loiza Aldea*. San Juan, 1954.

Allport, Gordon W. *The Nature of Prejudice*, abridged, pb. New York, 1958.

Alvarez Nazario, Manuel. *El elemento Afro-Negroide en el Español de Puerto Rico*. San Juan, 1961.

Anderson, Michael. *Approaches to the History of the Western Family, 1500–1914*. London, 1980.

Anderson, Rodney D. "Race and Social Stratification: A Comparison of Working-Class Spaniards, Indians, and Castas in Guadalajara, Mexico in 1821." *Hispanic American Historical Review* 68:2 (May 1988), 209–43.

Andrews, George Reid. *The Afro-Argentines of Buenos Aires, 1800–1900*. Madison, Wis., 1980.

——. *Blacks and Whites in São Paulo, Brazil*. Madison, Wis., 1991.

Aponte Torres, Gilberto. *San Mateo de Cangrejos: Notas para su historia*. San Juan, 1985.

Archer, Christon I. *The Army in Bourbon Mexico, 1760–1810*. Albuquerque, N.M., 1977.

Arriaga, Eduardo E. *Mortality Decline and Its Demographic Effects in Latin America*. Berkeley, 1970.

Arrom, Silvia Marina. *The Women of Mexico City, 1790–1857*. Stanford, Calif., 1985.

Ayala, José Antonio. *La masonería de obediencia Española en Puerto Rico en el siglo XIX*. Murcia, Spain, 1991.

Azize Vargas, Yamila, ed. *la mujer en Puerto Rico*. Río Piedras, P.R., 1987.

Banton, Michael. *Race Relations*. New York, 1967.

Baralt, Guillermo A. *Esclavos rebeldes: Conspiraciones y sublevaciones de esclavos en Puerto Rico (1795–1873)*. San Juan, 1981.

Barceló Miller, María T. "De la polilla a la virtud: Visión sobre la mujer de la Iglesia jerárquica de Puerto Rico." *la mujer en Puerto Rico*. Ed. Yamila Azize Vargas. Río Piedras, P.R., 1987. 49–84.

Bayle, Constantino. *Los cabildos seculares en América Española*. Madrid, 1952.

Benmayor, Rina, Ana Juarbe, Celia Alvarez, and Blanca Vázquez. *Stories to Live by: Continuity and Change in Three Generations of Puerto Rican Women*. New York, 1987.

Berlin, Ira. *Slaves Without Masters: The Free Negro in the Antebellum South*. New York, 1974.

Billingsley, Andrew. *Black Families in White America*, pb., New York, 1968.

——. *Climbing Jacob's Ladder: The Enduring Legacy of African-American Families*. New York, 1992.

Blanco, Tomás. *El prejuicio racial en Puerto Rico*, 2d ed. San Juan, 1948.

Bowser, Frederick P. *The African Slave in Colonial Peru, 1524–1650*. Stanford, Calif., 1974.

——. "The Free Person of Color in Mexico City and Lima: Manumission and Opportunity, 1580–1650." *Race and Slavery in the Western Hemisphere: Quantitative Studies.* Ed. Stanley L. Engerman and Eugene D. Genovese. Princeton, N.J., 1975. 331–68.

Brathwaite, Edward. *The Development of Creole Society in Jamaica, 1770–1820.* Oxford, 1971.

Braudel, Fernand. *The Wheels of Commerce,* vol. 2. In *Civilization and Capitalism 15th–18th Century,* 3 vols., tr. New York, 1982–1984.

Bronner, Fred. "Urban Society in Colonial Spanish America: Research Trends." *Latin American Research Review* 2:21 (1986), 7–72.

Buckely, Roger Norman. *Slaves in Red Coats: The British West India Regiments, 1795–1815.* New Haven, Conn., 1979.

Campos Esteve, Carmen. "La politica del Comercio: Los comerciantes de San Juan, 1837–1844." Master's thesis, University of Puerto Rico, 1987.

Caro Castro, Aida R. *El cabildo o régimen municipal Puertorriqueño en el siglo XVIII,* 2 vols. San Juan, 1974.

Carr, Raymond. *Puerto Rico: A Colonial Experiment.* New York, 1984.

Carroll, Patrick J. *Blacks in Colonial Veracruz: Race, Ethnicity, and Regional Development.* Austin, Tex., 1991.

Castro, María De Los Angeles. *Arquitectura en San Juan de Puerto Rico (siglo XIX).* Río Piedras, P.R., 1980.

Chance, John K. *Race and Class in Colonial Oaxaca.* Stanford, Calif., 1978.

——. "The Ecology of Race and Class in Late Colonial Oaxaca." *Studies in Spanish American Population History.* Ed. David J. Robinson. Boulder, Colo., 1981. 93–117.

Chance, John K. and William B. Taylor. "Estate and Class in a Colonial City: Oaxaca in 1792." *Comparative Studies in Society and History* 19:4 (Oct. 1977), 455–87.

——. "Estate and Class: A Reply." *Comparative Studies in Society and History* 21:3 (July 1979), 434–42.

Chardón, Carlos Fernando. *Reseña histórica de origin y desarrollo de las Milicias Disciplinadas Puertorriqueñas bajo el régimen Español (1511–1898).* San Juan, 1978.

Cohen, David W. and Jack P. Greene, eds. *Neither Slave nor Free: The Freedmen of African Descent in the Slave Societies of the New World.* Baltimore, Md., 1972.

Coll y Toste, Cayetano. *Historia de la esclavitud en Puerto Rico.* San Juan, 1969.

Colombán Rosario, José and Justina Carrión. *Problemas sociales: El negro, Haiti—Estados Unidos—Puerto Rico.* San Juan, 1940.

Cook, Sherburne F. and Woodrow Borah. *Essays in Population History*, 2 vols. Berkeley, Calif., 1971–1979.

Cope, R. Douglas. *The Limits of Racial Domination: Plebeian Society in Colonial Mexico City, 1660–1720.* Madison, Wis., 1994.

Corwin, Arthur F. "Afro-Brazilians: Myths and Realities." *Slavery and Race Relations in Latin America.* Ed. Robert Brent Toplin, pb. Westport, Conn., 1976. 385–437.

Coulthard, G. R. *Race and Colour in Caribbean Literature,* tr. London, 1962.

Cox, Edward L. *Free Coloreds in the Slave Societies of St. Kitts and Grenada, 1763–1833.* Knoxville, Tenn., 1984.

Cox, Oliver C. *Caste, Class, and Race: A Study in Social Dynamics.* New York, 1948.

Curet, José. "From Slave to *Liberto*: A Study on Slavery and its Abolition in Puerto Rico, 1840–1880." Ph.D. diss., Columbia University, 1980.

Curtin, Philip D. *Two Jamaicas: The Role of Ideas in a Tropical Colony.* Cambridge, Mass., 1955.

Curry, Leonard P. *The Free Black in Urban America, 1800–1850: The Shadow of the Dream.* Chicago, 1981.

Davis, David Brion. *The Problem of Slavery in Western Culture,* 2d rev. ed.; New York, 1988 [orig. pub. 1969].

Degler, Carl N. *Neither Black nor White: Slavery and Race Relations in Brazil and the United States.* New York, 1972.

Deschamps Chapeaux, Pedro. *El negro en la economía Habanera del siglo XIX.* Havana, 1971.

Díaz Quiñones, Arcadio. *el almuerzo en la hierba (lloérns torres, palés matos, rené marques).* Río Piedras, P.R., 1982.

Díaz Soler, Luis M. *Historia de la esclavitud negra en Puerto Rico,* 3d ed. n.p., 1970.

Diggs, Irene. "Color in Colonial Spanish America." *Journal of Negro History* 38 (1953), 403–27.

Dollard, John. *Caste and Class in a Southern Town,* 2d. ed. New York, 1949.

Drusine, Leon. "Some Factors in Anti-Negro Prejudice among Puerto Rican Boys in New York City." Ph.D. diss., New York University, 1955.

Dunn, Richard S. *Sugar and Slavery: The Rise of the Planter Class in the English West Indies, 1624–1713,* pb. New York, 1973.

Engerman, Stanley L. and Eugene D. Genovese, eds. *Race and Slavery in the Western Hemisphere: Quantitative Studies.* Princeton, N.J., 1975.

Fitzpatrick, Joseph P. *Puerto Rican Americans,* 2d ed. Englewood Cliffs, N.J., 1987.

Flores, Juan. *Divided Borders: Essays on Puerto Rican Identity.* Houston, Tex., 1993.

Franklin, John Hope. *The Free Negro in North Carolina, 1790–1860.* Chapel Hill, N.C., 1943.

Géigel de Gandía, Luisa. *La genealogía y el apellido de Campeche.* San Juan, 1972.

Goldberg, Marta B. "La población negra y mulata de la Ciudad de Buenos Aires, 1810–1840." *Desarrollo Económico* 61 (April–June 1976), 75–99.

González, José Luis. *El país de cuatro pisos y otros ensayos,* 6th ed. Río Piedras, P.R., 1987.

———. *The Four-Storyed Country and Other Essays,* tr. Maplewood, N.J., 1990.

González, José Luis and Mónica Mansour. *Poesía Negra de América.* México, D.F., 1976.

González Mendoza, Juan R. "The Parish of San Germán de Auxerre in Puerto Rico, 1765–1850: Patterns of Settlement and Development." Ph.D. diss., State University of New York at Stony Brook, 1989.

Goveia, Elsa V. *Slave Society in the British Leeward Islands at the End of the Eighteenth Century.* New Haven, Conn., 1965.

Graff, Harvey J. *The Literacy Myth and Social Structure in the Nineteenth-Century City.* New York, 1979.

Graham, Richard, ed. *The Idea of Race in Latin America, 1870–1940.* Austin, Tex., 1990.

Greenow, Linda. "Family, Household and Home: A Micro-Geographic Analysis of Cartagena (New Granada) in 1777." Discussion paper no. 18, Department of Geography, Syracuse University, 1976.

———. "Spatial Dimensions of Household and Family in Eighteenth-Century Spanish America." Discussion paper no. 35, Department of Geography, Syracuse University, 1977.

Hacker, Andrew. *Two Nations: Black and White, Separate, Hostile, Unequal,* pb. New York, 1993.

Hajnal, J. "European Marriage Patterns in Perspective." *Population in History.* Ed. D. V. Glass and D. E. C. Eversley. London, 1965. 101–43.

Hall, Gwendolyn Midlo. *Social Control in Slave Plantation Societies: A Comparison of St. Domingue and Cuba.* Baltimore, Md., 1971.

Handler, Jerome S. *The Unappropriated People: Freedmen In the Slave Society of Barbados.* Baltimore, Md., 1974.

Harris, Marvin. *Patterns of Race in the Americas.* New York, 1964.

Helg, Aline. *Our Rightful Share: The Afro-Cuban Struggle for Equality, 1886–1912.* Chapel Hill, N.C., 1995.

Henriques, Fernando. *Family and Colour in Jamaica,* 2d ed. London, 1968.

Herschberg, Theodore. "Free-Born and Slave-Born Blacks in Antebellum Philadelphia in 1847." *Race and Slavery in the Western Hemisphere.* Ed. Stanley L. Engerman and Eugene D. Genovese. Princeton, N.J., 1975.

Heuman, Gad J. *Between Black and White: Race, Politics, and the Free Coloreds in Jamaica, 1792–1865.* Westport, Conn., 1981.

Higman, B. W. *Slave Population and Economy in Jamaica, 1807–1834.* Cambridge, Eng., 1976.

Hoetink, H. *The Two Variants in Caribbean Race Relations,* tr. New York, 1967.

——. *Slavery and Race Relations in the Americas: Comparative Notes on Their Nature and Nexus.* New York, 1973.

Hostos, Adolfo de. *Historia de San Juan: Ciudad murada, 1521–1898.* San Juan, 1966.

Hünefeldt, Christine. *Paying the Price of Freedom: Family and Labor among Lima's Slaves,* 1800–1854. Berkeley, Calif., 1994.

Iglesias, César Andreu, ed. *Memoirs of Bernardo Vega: A Contribution to the History of the Puerto Rican Community in New York.* New York, 1984.

Jackson, Luther Porter. *Free Negro Labor and Property Holding in Virginia, 1830–1860,* 2d ed. New York, 1969.

Johnson, Lyman L. "Manumission in Colonial Buenos Aires, 1776–1810." *HAHR* 59:2 (May 1979), 258–79.

——. "Artisans." *Cities and Society in Colonial Latin America.* Ed. Louisa Schell Hoberman and Susan Midgen Socolow. Albuquerque, N.M., 1986. 227–50.

Jopling, Carol F. *Puerto Rican Houses in Sociohistorical Perspective.* Knoxville, Tenn., 1988.

Jordan, Winthrop D. "American Chiaroscuro: The Status and Definition of Mulattoes in the British Colonies." *William and Mary Quarterly* 19 (April 1962), 183–200.

——. *White over Black: American Attitudes toward the Negro, 1550–1812,* pb. Baltimore, Md., 1969.

Jorge, Angela. "The Black Puerto Rican Woman in Contemporary American Society." *The Puerto Rican Woman: Perspectives on Culture, History, and Society,* 2d ed. Ed. Edna Acosta-Bélen. New York, 1986. 180–87.

Katz, Michael B. "Occupational Classification in History." *Journal of Inter-disciplinary History* 3 (1972), 63–88.

Kinsbruner, Jay. "The Pulperos of Caracas and San Juan during the First Half of the Nineteenth Century." *Latin American Reseach Review* 13:1 (1978), 65–85.

———. *Petty Capitalism in Spanish America: The Pulperos of Puebla, Mexico City, Caracas and Buenos Aires.* Dellplain Latin American Studies, no. 21. Ed. David J. Robinson. Boulder, Colo., 1987.

———. *Independence in Spanish America: Civil Wars, Revolutions, and Underdevelopment.* Albuquerque, N.M., 1994.

Klein, Herbert S. *Slavery in the Americas: A Comparative Study of Virginia and Cuba.* Chicago, 1967.

———. *African Slavery in Latin America and the Caribbean.* New York, 1986.

Knight, Alan. "Racism, Revolution, and *Indigenismo*: Mexico, 1910–1940." *The Idea of Race in Latin America, 1870–1940.* Ed. Richard Graham. Austin, Tex., 1990. 71–113.

Knight, Franklin W. and Colin A. Palmer, eds. *The Modern Caribbean.* Chapel Hill, N.C., 1989.

Kuethe, Allan J. *Cuba, 1753–1815: Crown, Military, and Society.* Knoxville, Tenn., 1986.

———. "The Status of the Free Pardo in the Disciplined Militia of New Granada." *Journal of Negro History* 56:2 (1971), 105–18.

Kuznesof, Elizabeth Anne. *Household Economy and Urban Development: São Paulo, 1765 to 1836.* Dellplain Latin American Studies, no. 18. Ed. David J. Robinson. Boulder, Colo., 1986.

———. "Household and Family Studies." *Latinas of the Americas.* Ed. K. Lynn Stoner. New York, 1989. 305–37.

Kuznesof, Elizabeth Anne and Robert Oppenheimer. "The Family and Society in Nineteenth-Century Latin America: An Historiographical Introduction." *Journal of Family History* 10:3 (fall 1985), 215–35.

Lanning, John Tate. "Legitimacy and *Limpieza de Sangre* in the Practice of Medicine in the Spanish Empire." *Jahrbuch für Geschichte von Staat Wirtschaft und Gesellschaft Lateinamericas* 4 (1967), 37–60.

Laslett, Peter, ed. *Household and Family in Past Time: Comparative Studies in the Size and Structure of the Domestic Group over the Last Three Centuries in England, France, Serbia, Japan, and Colonial North America.* Cambridge, Eng., 1974.

Larrazábal Blanco, Carlos. *Los negros y la esclavitud en Santo Domingo.* Santo Domingo, 1967.

Leach, E. R., ed. *Aspects of Caste in South India, Ceylon and North-West Pakistan.* Cambridge, Eng., 1960.

Lewis, Gordon K. *Puerto Rico: Freedom and Power in the Caribbean,* pb. New York, 1963.

Lewis, Oscar. *La Vida: A Puerto Rican Family in the Culture of Poverty— San Juan and New York.* New York, 1965.

Litwack, Leon F. *North of Slavery: The Negro in the Free States, 1790–1860.* Chicago, 1961.

Livi-Bacci, Massimo. *A History of Italian Fertility during the Last Two Centuries.* Princeton, N.J., 1977.

Lombardi, John V. *People and Places in Colonial Venezuela.* Bloomington, Ind., 1976.

Longres Jr., John F. "Racism and Its Effects on Puerto Rican Continentals." *Social Casework* 55:2 (Feb. 1974), 67–75.

Love, Edgar J. "Marriage Patterns of Persons of African Descent in a Colonial Mexico City Parish." *Hispanic American Historical Review* 51:1 (Feb. 1971), 79–91.

Martinez-Alier, Verena. *Marriage, Class and Colour in Nineteenth-Century Cuba,* pb. Cambridge, Eng., 1974.

Mathews, Thomas M. "The Question of Color in Puerto Rico." *Slavery and Race Relations in Latin America,* pb. Ed. Robert Brent Toplin. Westport, Conn., 1976. 299–323.

Matos, Félix V. "Economy, Society and Urban Life: Women in Nineteenth Century, San Juan, Puerto Rico (1820–1870)." Ph.D. diss., Columbia University, 1994.

——. "Street Vendors, Pedlars, Shop-Owners and Domestics: Some Aspects of Women's Economic Roles in Nineteenth-Century San Juan, Puerto Rico (1820–1870)." *Engendering History: Caribbean Women in Historical Perspective.* Ed. Verene Shepherd, et al. New York, 1995. 176–93.

Mattoso, Katia M. De Queirós. *To Be a Slave in Brazil, 1550–1888,* tr. New Brunswick, N.J., 1986.

McAlister, Lyle N. *The "Fuero Militar" in New Spain, 1764–1800.* Gainesville, Fla., 1957.

McCaa, Robert. "Women's Position, Family and Fertility Decline in Parral (Mexico) 1777–1930." *Annales de Démographie Historique* (1989), 233–43.

——, ed. *Journal of Family History* 16:3 (1991).

McCaa, Robert and Stuart B. Schwartz. "Measuring Marriage Patterns: Percentages, Cohen's Kappa, and Log-Linear Models." *Comparative Studies in Society and History* 25 (1983), 711–20.

McCaa, Robert, Stuart B. Schwartz, and Arturo Grubessich. "Race and Class in Colonial Latin America: A Critique." *Comparative Studies in Society and History* 21 (July 1979), 421–33.

Mendoza, Antonio C. *Historia de la educación en Puerto Rico (1512–1826)*. Washington, D.C., 1937.

Mills, C. Wright, Clarence Senior, and Rose Kohn Goldsen. *The Puerto Rican Journey: New York's Newest Migrants*. New York, 1950.

Mintz, Sidney W. "Puerto Rico: An Essay in the Definition of a National Culture." *Status of Puerto Rico: Selected Background Studies Prepared for the United States–Puerto Rico Commission on the Status of Puerto Rico*. Washington, D.C., 1966.

Mintz, Sidney W. and Richard Price. *The Birth of African-American Culture: An Anthropological Perspective*. Boston, Mass., 1992.

Mizio, Emelicia. "Impact of External Systems on the Puerto Rican Family." *Social Casework* 55:2 (Feb. 1974), 76–83.

Moore, John Preston. *The Cabildo in Peru under the Hapsburgs*. Durham, N.C., 1954.

——. *The Cabildo in Peru under the Bourbons*. Durham, N.C., 1966.

Morales Carrión, Arturo, ed. *Puerto Rico: A Political and Cultural History*. New York, 1983.

Moreno, José Luis. "La estructura social y demográfica de la Ciudad de Buenos Aires en el año 1778." *Anuario del Instituto de Investigaciones Históricas* (Universidad Nacional del Litoral, Rosario, Argentina) 8 (1965), 151–70.

Mörner, Magnus. *Race Mixture in the History of Latin America*. Boston, Mass., 1967.

——, ed. *Race and Class in Latin America*. New York, 1971.

——. "Classes, Strata and Elites: The Social Historian's Dilemma." *Classes, Strata And Elites: Essays on Social Stratification in Nordic and Third World History*. Ed. Magnus Mörner and Thommy Svensson. Göteborg, Sweden, 1988. 3–50.

Newell, Colin. *Methods and Models in Demography*. London, 1988.

Nistal-Moret, Benjamín. "El Pueblo de Nuestra Señora de la Candalaria y del Apostal San Matías de Manatí, 1800–1880: Its Ruling Classes and the Institution of Black Slavery." Ph.D. diss., State University of New York, Stony Brook, 1977.

——, ed. *Esclavos prófugos y cimarrones: Puerto Rico, 1770–1870*. Río Piedras, P.R., 1984.

Osuna, Juan José. *A History of Education in Puerto Rico*. Río Piedras, P.R., 1949.

Padilla, Elena. *Up from Puerto Rico*. New York, 1958.

Padilla, Felix. *Puerto Rican Chicago*. Notre Dame, Ind., 1987.

Palmer, Colin. "Identity, Race, and Black Power in Independent Jamaica." *The Modern Caribbean*. Ed. Franklin W. Knight and Colin A. Palmer. Chapel Hill, N.C., 1989. 111–28.

Paquette, Robert L. *Sugar Is Made with Blood: The Conspiracy of La Escalera and the Conflict between Empires over Slavery in Cuba*. Middletown, Conn., 1988.

Patterson, Orlando. *The Sociology of Slavery: An Analysis of the Origins, Development and Structure of Negro Slave Society in Jamaica*. London, 1967.

——. *Slavery and Social Death: A Comparative Study*. Cambridge, Mass., 1982.

Picó, Fernando. *Libertad y servidumbre en el Puerto Rico del siglo XIX*, 2d ed., rev. San Juan, 1982.

——. "La demografía histórica y la historia de la Iglesia: Perspectivas para la historia de la Iglesia Católica en Puerto Rico." *Punto y Coma* 1:1 (1988), 37–41.

——. *Vivir en Caimito*, 2d ed. Río Piedras, P.R., 1989.

——. *Historia general de Puerto Rico*, 5th ed. Río Piedras, P.R., 1990.

Picó de Hernández, Isabel. "The History of Women's Struggle for Equality in Puerto Rico." *The Puerto Rican Woman*. Ed. Edna Acosta-Belén. New York, 1986. 25–37.

Plakans, Andrejs and Charles Wetherell. "The Kinship Domain in an Eastern European Peasant Community: Pinkenhof, 1833–1850." *American Historical Review* 93:2 (April 1988), 359–86.

Pressat, Roland. *Population*, tr. London, 1970.

——. *Demographie statistique*. Paris, 1972.

Rainwater, Lee and William L. Yancey, eds. *The Moynihan Report and the Politics of Controversy*. Cambridge, Mass., 1967.

Rama, Carlos M. *Los Afro-Uruguayos de Montevideo: El siglo ilustrado*, 3d ed. Montevideo, 1969.

Ramos, Donald. "Marriage and the Family in Colonial Vila Rica." *Hispanic American Historical Review* 55:2 (May 1975), 200–25.

——. "Vila Rica: Profile of a Colonial Brazilian Urban Center." *The Americas* 35:4 (April 1979), 495–526.

Rigdon, Susan M. *The Culture Facade: Art, Science, and Politics in the Work of Oscar Lewis*. Urbana, Ill., 1988.

Rivera Ayala, Noel. "Las Milicias Disciplinadas Puertorriqueñas: Grandes períodos y el duradero valor de la institución (1765–1850)." Master's thesis, University of Puerto Rico, 1978.

Robinson, David J. "The Analysis of Eighteenth-Century Spanish American Cities: Some Problems and Alternative Solutions." Discussion paper no. 4, Department of Geography, Syracuse University, 1975.

Robinson, David J. and Michael M. Swann. "Geographical Interpretations of the Hispanic-American Colonial City: A Case Study of Caracas in the Late Eighteenth Century." *Latin America: Search for Geographical Explanations.* Ed. Robert J. Tata. Chapel Hill, N.C., 1976.

Rodríguez, Clara E. *Puerto Ricans: Born in the USA.* Boston, Mass., 1989.

Rodriguez-Cortes, Carmen N. "Social Practices of Ethnic Identity among Puerto Rican Students." Ph.D. diss., Columbia University, 1987.

Rodríguez Cruz, Juan. "Las relaciones raciales en Puerto Rico." *Revista de Ciencias Sociales* 9:4 (1965), 373–86.

Rodríguez León, Mario A. *Los regristros parroquiales y la microhistoria demográfica en Puerto Rico.* San Juan, 1990.

Rogler, Charles C. "The Role of Semantics in the Study of Race Distance in Puerto Rico." *Social Forces* 22 (Oct. 1943–May 1944), 448–53.

Rosenblat, Angel. *La población indígena y el mestizaje en América,* 2 vols. Buenos Aires, 1954.

Rout, Leslie B. *The African Experience in Spanish America.* Cambridge, Eng., 1976.

Ruggles, Steven. *Prolonged Connections: The Rise of the Extended Family in Nineteenth-Century England and America.* Madison, Wis., 1987.

Russell-Wood, A. J. R. *The Black Man in Slavery and Freedom in Colonial Brazil.* New York, 1982.

Rust, Philip F. and Patricia Seed. "Equality of Endogamy: Statistical Approaches." *Social Science Research* 14 (1985), 57–79.

Samayoa Guevara, Humberto. *Los gremios de artesanos en la Ciudad de Guatemala (1524–1821).* Guatemala City, 1962.

Sánchez Korrol, Virginia E. *From Colonia to Community: The History of Puerto Ricans in New York City,* 2d. ed. Berkeley, 1994.

Santana, Arturo. "Puerto Rico in a Revolutionary World." *Puerto Rico: A Political and Cultural History.* Ed. Arturo Morales Carrión. New York, 1983. 51–78.

Saunders, A. C. De C. M. *A Social History of Black Slaves and Freedmen in Portugal, 1441–1555.* Cambridge, Eng., 1982.

Scarano, Francisco A. *Sugar and Slavery in Puerto Rico: The Municipality of Ponce, 1815–1849.* Madison, Wis., 1984.

Schwartz, Stuart B. *Sugar Plantations in the Formation of Brazilian Society: Bahia, 1550–1835,* pb. Cambridge, Eng., 1989.

Seda Bonilla, Eduardo. "Dos modelos de relaciones raciales." *Mundo Nuevo* 3:31 (Jan. 1969), 29–43.

Seed, Patricia. "Social Dimensions of Race: Mexico City, 1753." *Hispanic American Historical Review* 62:4 (Nov. 1982), 569–606.

Seed, Patricia and Philip F. Rust. "Estate and Class in Colonial Oaxaca Revisited." *Comparative Studies in Society and History* 25 (1983), 703–10.

——. "Across the Pages with Estate and Class." *Comparative Studies in Society and History* 25 (1983), 721–24.

Sepúlveda-Rivera, Aníbal. "San Juan de Puerto Rico: Growth of a Caribbean Capital City." Ph.D. diss., Cornell University, 1986.

——. *San Juan: Historia de su desarrollo urbano, 1508–1898*. San Juan, 1989.

Sereno, Renzo. "Cryptomelanism: A Study of Color Relations and Personal Insecurity in Puerto Rico." *Psychiatry* 10 (1947), 261–69.

Sharp, William F. *Slavery on the Spanish Frontier: The Colombian Chaco, 1680–1810*. Norman, Okla., 1976.

Shepherd, Verene, et al., eds. *Engendering History: Caribbean Women in Historical Perspective*. New York, 1995.

Siegal, Arthur, Harold Orlans, and Loyal Greer. *Puerto Ricans in Philadelphia*, reprint ed. New York, 1975.

Stoner, K. Lynn, ed. *Latinas of the Americas: A Source Book*. New York, 1989.

Suárez Díaz, Ada. *El Doctor Ramón Emeterio Betances y la abolición de la esclavitud*, 2d ed. San Juan, 1980.

Sued Badillo, Jalil and Angel López Cantos. *Puerto Rico Negro*. Río Piedras, P.R., 1986.

Swann, Michael. *Tierra Adentro: Settlement and Society in Colonial Durango. Dellplain Latin American Studies*, no. 10. Ed. David J. Robinson. Boulder, Colo., 1982.

——. *Migrants in the Mexican North: Mobility, Economy, and Society in a Colonial World. Dellplain Latin American Studies*, no. 24. Ed. David J. Robinson. Boulder, Colo., 1989.

Szuchman, Mark D. "Household Structure and Political Crisis: Buenos Aires, 1810–1860." *Latin American Research Review* 21:3 (1986), 55–93.

——. *Order, Family, and Community in Buenos Aires, 1810–1860*. Stanford, Calif., 1988.

Taeuber, Karl E. and Alma F. Taeuber. *Negroes in Cities: Residential Segregation and Neighborhood Change*, pb. New York, 1969.

Toplin, Robert Brent, ed. *Slavery and Race Relations in Latin America*, pb. Westport, Conn., 1976.

Toplin, Robert Brent. *Freedom and Prejudice: The Legacy of Slavery in the United States and Brazil.* Westport, Conn., 1981.

Torruellas, Rosa M. "Learning English in Three Private Schools in Puerto Rico: Issues of Class, Identity and Ideology." Ph.D. diss., New York University, 1990.

Tuden, Arthur and Leonard Plotnicov, eds. *Social Stratification in Africa.* New York, 1970.

Tumin, Melvin M. *Social Class and Social Change in Puerto Rico,* 2d ed. Indianapolis, Ind., 1971.

Valdes, Dennis N. "The Decline of the *Sociedad de Castas* in Mexico City." Ph.D. diss., University of Michigan, 1978.

Van den Berghe, Pierre L. "Race, Class, and Ethnicity in South Africa." *Social Stratification in Africa.* Ed. Arthur Tuden and Leonard Plotnicov. New York, 1970. 345–71.

——. *Race and Ethnicity: Essays in Comparative Sociology.* New York, 1970.

Van Dijk, Teun A. *Prejudice in Discourse.* Amsterdam and Philadelphia, 1984.

Vásquez Calzada, José L. *La población de Puerto Rico y su trayectoria histórica.* Río Piedras, P.R., 1988.

Wade, Peter. "Race and class: The case of South American Blacks." *Ethnic and Racial Studies* 8:2 (April 1985), 233–49.

——. *Blackness and Race Mixture: The Dynamics of Racial Identity in Colombia.* Baltimore, Md., 1993.

Waldron, Kathleen. "A Social History of a Primate City: The Case of Caracas, 1750–1810." Ph.D. diss., Indiana University, 1977.

Wright, Winthrop R. "Elitist Attitudes toward Race in Twentieth-Century Venezuela." *Slavery and Race Relations in Latin America.* Ed. Robert Brent Toplin. Westport, Conn., 1976, 1993. 325–47.

——. *Café con leche: Race, Class, and National Image in Venezuela,* pb. Austin, Tex., 1993.

Wrigley, E. A. *Population and History.* New York, 1969.

Zapatero, Juan Manuel. "De la Batalla del Caribe: El ultimo ataque Inglés a Puerto Rico (17 de Abril a 1 de Mayo de 1797)." *Historia Militar* 3 (1959), 91–134.

Zenon Cruz, Isabelo. *Narciso descubre su trasero: El negro en la cultura Puertorriqueña,* 2d ed. Humacao, P.R., 1975.

Index

Jay Kinsbruner is Professor of History at Queens College and Graduate Center, CUNY